# MOSCOW

## HISTORY, ART AND ARCHITECTURE

Text
Kathleen Berton Murrell

**FLINT RIVER PRESS**
London

D1380009

# Moscow, History, Art and Architecture

© Flint River Press Ltd, 1995

ISBN 1 871489 22 9

*Photographs by*

Andrea Luppi

Otto Pohl

*Design*

Gane Aleksic

*Editor*

Madge Phillips

Typesetting by Avalon

Organisation by Eurocity Associates Ltd, London

Printed in Slovenia byTiskarna Ljudska Pravica, Ljubljana

# CONTENTS

# THE KREMLIN

Moscow is not built on a grid pattern like New York, nor is it composed of small lanes and winding main roads like London. It has developed historically into an attractive circular-radial pattern with main roads emanating from the central core — the Kremlin — intersected by narrow lanes and broad circular avenues. This unusual geometry is further enhanced by the shape of the Kremlin itself, a rough triangle fitting comfortably on its hilly site, at first entirely surrounded by water. The flow of the Neglinnaya River (now in conduits) defended the north-western flank, a moat protected the eastern, Red Square side, and the Moskva River took care of the third, southern edge.

The Kremlin (Russian *kreml* = citadel) is the very heart of Moscow. With its more than thirty golden cupolas, its ancient churches and tall bell tower, its palaces and government offices, it is the most important place not only architecturally but historically and politically in the whole city. The original fortress on this site, raised in the twelfth century by Prince Yuri Dolgoruki, was a wooden structure surrounded by a palisade. Its walls and two important churches were built of stone at the time of Ivan Kalita in the middle of the fourteenth century. But it was under his grandson, Dmitry Donskoi, the first Russian to inflict a defeat on the Tartar-Mongol invaders, that the Kremlin assumed its present size. A century later, in the 1480s, it was rebuilt under Ivan III, and since then the walls and main cathedrals have not been substantially altered. This unique complex of churches, palaces, museums and offices remains to this day the hub of political life — here Yeltsin took over the office occupied before him by Gorbachev, Khrushchev and Stalin. In 1990 it again became the focus of the Russian Orthodox Church. And as a tourist attraction it is unrivalled.

After a period of near anarchy and feuding among competing princes, by the 1470s, under the Grand Prince Ivan III, Moscow, or rather the principality of Muscovy as it was then called in the West, had risen to the foremost position among the central Russian city states. Moscow's hegemony was indicated in 1328 when the Metropolitan of All Russia, Peter, moved his residency from Vladimir, devastated by repeated Mongol-Tartar attacks, to Moscow. In 1395 an even more auspicious event occurred when the holy icon, the twelfth-century Virgin of Vladimir, was brought to Moscow. The icon depicts the Virgin as a young mother lovingly bending her head to the child, who sweetly strokes her cheek. It is difficult to overemphasise the political importance of this icon — for the illiterate Russian population, the arrival of its most ancient and sacred image was decisive in confirming Moscow's pre-eminence. It also seemed to thwart an expected attack by the Tartars under Tamerlane; inexplicably, just after the arrival of the icon the warlord turned back on reaching the Muscovite lands.

With a strong prince, Ivan III, on the throne, Moscow's future was assured. Ivan further enhanced his prestige and authority by marrying the niece of the last Byzantine emperor (Byzantium had fallen to the Turks in 1453). She had been educated in Rome in the Catholic faith and was brought to Moscow to the horror of the narrow-minded Orthodox Muscovites. Nevertheless, the marriage (in the Orthodox rite) established Ivan's claim to be the protector of the Orthodox Church and Moscow's title of the 'Third Rome', the first two having fallen to the barbarians and

*1. The 15th-century Kremlin towers — the corner Arsenal, the Gothic Nicholas, the small Senate and the grand Saviour — confront Red Square, guarding the 1787 Senate with its round dome.*

the infidel. At this time, too, Ivan adopted the Byzantine double-headed eagle as the royal emblem and the title of 'tsar' (from caesar).

Ivan III considered one of his main tasks the renewal of the Kremlin, which had fallen into decay during the wars between the grand princes. Typically, after Russian builders proved their incompetence, he looked to Italy, then experiencing the exhilaration of the Renaissance, for master-builders and architects. The broad brick walls, five main gates and twenty towers surrounding the Kremlin were built (1485-95) by Italian masters in the distinctive north Italian style. The merlons — Russians say swallow-tails — at the tops of the walls strongly recall the Castello Sforzesco in Milan. The distinctive tent-shaped summits to the towers were not added until the seventeenth century. The five gates were later surmounted by imperial double-headed eagles, which surprisingly remained in place until well into the 1930s, when Soviet symbols, huge ruby-coloured glass stars, were erected in their place.

**Cathedral of the Assumption** (*Uspensky Sobor*)  Aristotle Fioravanti, an engineer from Bologna, was the most talented of the immigrant Italians. His task was the construction of the principal church of the Kremlin, the Cathedral of the Assumption. The feast to celebrate Mary's assumption into heaven, also known as the Dormition, was and is one of the most important and popular festivals in the Russian Church. Fioravanti, using the great twelfth-century cathedral at Vladimir as his model, was able to erect the remarkable church in Cathedral Square in only four years (1475-79). It is virtually unchanged to this day. A belt of blind arcading masks windows which make the interior unusually light. Russian influence is seen in the five heavy gold cupolas, not yet thoroughly onion-shaped, which rise from the roof. Italian influence is evident in the discrete apse almost hidden within the cuboid — Russian church builders invariably preferred a more voluptuously rounded east end. Inside, uncluttered by seating arrangements, it is unusually airy and spacious and full of colour, every section of wall, even the insides of the high cupolas, painted with monumental seventeenth-century frescoes (remnants of the original frescoes are in the altar). At the eastern end rises the tiered iconostasis (altar screen) of ancient icons. Although the cathedral was Fioravanti's masterpiece, he got scant thanks. Accused of financial irregularities, he was thrown into prison, where he eventually died, still begging to return to his beloved Italy.

Tombs of the metropolitans and patriarchs with brass covers line the walls. A superb collection of ancient icons taken from cities vanquished by the Moscow princes is displayed, including the twelfth-century St George from Novgorod, and the Saviour with the Angry Eye (Moscow, fifteenth century). The most precious icon, the Virgin of Vladimir, was removed to the Tretyakov Gallery in 1918, but a fifteenth-century copy can be seen to the left of the iconostasis.

The cathedral has been witness to many historic occasions. Here, in 1480, Ivan III formally tore up the charter under which tribute was paid to the Tartars. Here, too, in 1568, Ivan the Terrible was sharply denounced by Metropolitan Philip, in return for which Philip was brutally arrested while at prayer in the cathedral. He was later murdered by Ivan's henchmen. In 1812, as the French began their undignified retreat, Napoleon ordered the Kremlin to be blown up (damaging only walls and towers) and the confiscation of valuable gold and silver plate; the Cossacks who harassed the fleeing French and recovered the plate pre-

*3. The colourful, ridged onion domes enhance the exotic appearance of St Basil's Cathedral in Red Square.*

*4. On 31 December 1991, the Soviet red flag was lowered from the Senate roof and replaced by the new Russian flag, formerly the flag of the tsarist merchant navy.*

*5. The tsars doffed their hats as they passed under the icon (now removed) on the Saviour Gate, the formal entrance to the Kremlin.*

sented the cathedral with the large heavy chandelier made out of the stolen silver. All coronations of the Russian monarchs after Ivan III and up to and including Nicholas II took place in the cathedral. And here, in 1913, Nicholas II celebrated with pomp and ceremony the three-hundredth anniversary of the Romanov dynasty, little knowing that within five years the dynasty would be overthrown and he and his whole family murdered.

**Faceted Palace** (*Granovitaya Palata*) To the left of the Assumption Cathedral is the oldest surviving secular building of the Kremlin, the Faceted Palace, so named because of the diamond-shaped stonework on the façade. It was built (1487-91) by two Italians, Marco Ruffo and Pietro Antonio Solario, but has been altered over the centuries; its original high-pitched gilded roof has made way for one of lower height, and the Venetian windows were added in the seventeenth century. The magnificent staircase known as the Red Porch was removed in the 1930s, when a mundane dining-room was made for delegates to Communist Party congresses. In 1994 it was rebuilt by order of President Yeltsin.

The Faceted Palace still contains the original grand throne room and banqueting hall with its magnificent central pillar supporting the groin-vaulted ceiling. The painted walls and vaulting were done in the 1880s to a seventeenth-century design. Even the elaborate plasterwork on the pillar and doorways has been thoroughly restored, the whole giving an impression of opulent splendour. It was used for church councils, for meetings of boyars, and other councils of state, and for banquets, feasts and reception of ambassadors — it was probably here that the English adventurer, Richard Chancellor, was received by Ivan the Terrible in 1553. In recent times elaborate banquets have again been staged in the palace for visiting dignitaries — in the Eighties, Prime Minister

6. Lenin's classical mausoleum (designed by Alexei Shchusev, 1929) in front of the Senate Tower. Trotsky's memoirs recall the imperial double-headed eagle still on the gate in the 1920s.

7. St Nicholas the Wonderworker is one of Russia's most popular saints, patron of sailors, farmers and weavers. He is often the subject of frescoes and, as here, icons. This 16th-century icon is of the Novgorod School.

Margaret Thatcher and President Reagan, and in 1994, Queen Elizabeth II of Britain.

**Cathedral of the Annunciation** (*Blagoveshchensky Sobor*)  The richly adorned Annunciation Cathedral, next to the Faceted Palace, was erected (1484-89) under Ivan III by master-builders from Pskov. (Pskov, on the western border of Muscovy, escaped the Tartar yoke because of its remote position). Its nine gold cupolas shine brightly in the late afternoon sun and its position, close to the Moskva River, ensures that it can be seen from many vantage points in the south of the city. Built over the crypt of an earlier church, it is high off the ground up a flight of steps. In the sixteenth century, its open gallery was enclosed, domes were added to the four corners of the gallery, and two more false domes placed on the roof to balance the original three. All nine were covered with gold sheet. Smaller than the Assumption and Archangel Cathedrals, it served as the chapel royal of the tsars, where marriages, christenings and other services were held. It is said that Ivan the Terrible, when he exceeded the statutory three wives allowed by the Orthodox Church, was forbidden by the brave Metropolitan Philip (later murdered by Ivan) from attending services in the chapel and had to stand behind a grille on the south-east side.

Inside the narrow and close chamber, magnificent frescoes cover every inch of wall and column, the colours reflected in the stone floor of red and brown jasper. The tall iconostasis in front of the altar that dominates the narrow room is the most splendid in Russia. Some of the icons date from 1405, and were painted by the most outstanding artists ever to have worked in Russia: Theophanes the Greek, Prokhor of Gorodets, and

the inimitable Andrei Rublev. Especially remarkable is the Deesis composition in the main row, where Theophanes painted Christ in Majesty with the Virgin Mary on his right and John the Baptist on his left. Rublev is credited with some of the delightful paintings of the third, smaller tier of the major festivals of the church. These paintings miraculously survived many fires, including the exceptionally bad one of 1547. In the Soviet period, although the church was closed for services, the icons were meticulously cleaned and maintained.

**Cathedral of the Archangel Michael** (*Arkhangelsky Sobor*) The Archangel Cathedral, the third of the major churches of the Kremlin, is situated high on the bank of the Moskva River, opposite the golden-headed Annunciation Cathedral. Built (1505-09) by Alevisio Novi of Venice,

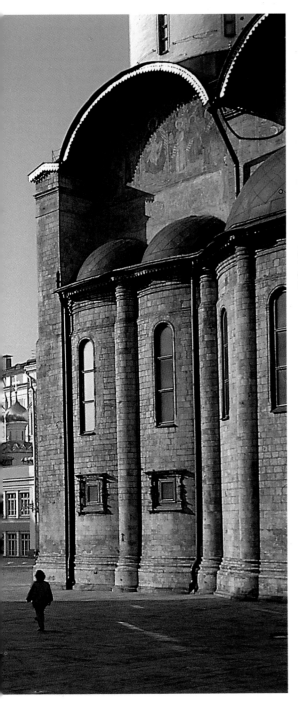

*9. Although nearly half were destroyed in the Stalin and Khrushchev eras, Moscow still has a large number of churches, including many of the early period.*

it displays more Italian characteristics than the other churches. The large 'shells' that complete the vertical wall divisions — later to become a popular device in Russian architecture — and pilasters with Corinthian capitals appear for the first time in this church.

The Archangel Michael was the protector of royalty and the cathedral was used as the burial place for the Moscow grand princes starting with Ivan Kalita in 1349 and ending with Peter II, who died in Moscow in 1730. With the exceptions of Boris Godunov and Nicholas II, all the other tsars, including Peter the Great, are buried in the Peter-Paul Fortress in St Petersburg; Godunov is buried at the Trinity-Sergius Monastery north of Moscow and the remains of Nicholas have only recently been identified in a mine shaft near Yekaterinburg.

*10. Sculpture of Lev Tolstoy by A. Portyanko (1972) near the wooden house where he and his family lived for 20 winters in the unfashionable Khamovniki factory district.*

The tsars' stone sarcophagi with brass covers added in 1903 fill most of the space within the cathedral. Underneath, in the basement, lie the grand princesses, removed from the Ascension Convent when that was destroyed in the 1930s. Ivan the Terrible is buried within the altar. The remains of little Prince Dmitry, murdered in Uglich allegedly by agents of Boris Godunov, are in a canopied tomb on the right.

**Church of the Deposition of the Robe** (*Rizopolozheniya Tserkov*) A small, white church by the western entrance of the Assumption Cathedral was the private chapel of the metropolitans, who served as head of the Russian Church until 1589, when the patriarchate was established. Built (1485) by Pskov master-builders, it contrasts sharply with the grand Italian-influenced cathedrals in its simplicity and size; in the

11. The Worker and the Peasant by G. Alexeev (1918) over the entrance to the Lenin Museum (formerly the Duma) was part of Lenin's Plan of Monumental Propaganda.

12. The Trinity Tower of the Kremlin, detail.

13. The upper part of the 15th-century Trinity Tower, one of the five main gates of the Kremlin, is a 17th-century addition. The Palace of Congresses behind (1961) is the only modern building in the Kremlin.

cramped interior the iconostasis takes up most of the space.

**Terem Palace** (*Teremnoi Dvorets*)  In the seventeenth century the Church of the Deposition of the Robe was attached by passageway to the Tsar's or Terem Palace, which since the l850s has been hidden within the body of the Grand Kremlin Palace. There are few hints of its presence, although the upper part of the Terem Palace, the steeply pitched peach and white roof, is sometimes glimpsed from the Old Stone Bridge. Above the passageway linking the metropolitan's church to the old palaces are eleven dazzling gold cupolas with drums of bright ceramic tiles, the outer manifestation of several small palace chapels. The Terem Palace was rebuilt in the first half of the seventeenth century incorporating the remnants of fifteenth- and sixteenth-century palaces. Little used after the capital was moved to St Petersburg, the ornate rooms with

15

strongly coloured tiled stoves were redecorated and heavily restored in the 1880s in a distinctive neo-Russian style.

**Ivan the Great Bell Tower** (*Kolokolnya Ivan Veliky*) By the early 1500s, three sides of the square boasted grand cathedrals; the fourth, east side, gave it vertical thrust with the construction of the tall bell tower known as Ivan the Great (Ivan Veliky). The present complex structure with its tall tower, cupolas and smaller bell tower (*zvonnitsa*) was built over a long period. The first, south tower, erected by Italian builders (1505-08) was extended to its present height of 81 metres by Boris Godunov at the end of the century, a landmark that could be seen for miles around. The central part of the bell tower, the belfry, was added in 1543; the great Resurrection Bell can be seen hanging below the onion

dome. The final section, the Filaret annexe, built in 1624, was badly damaged by explosives set by the retreating soldiers of Napoleon in 1812; it was partially rebuilt in classical style. After the Revolution, the 21 bells of Ivan the Great were silenced, although they rang for the victory parade in June 1945. Since 1990 their thrilling sound has been heard more frequently to announce solemn religious festivals in the Assumption Cathedral and at the Easter midnight service.

**Cathedral of the Twelve Apostles** (*Sobor Dvenadtsati Apostolov*) Slightly to the north of the Assumption Cathedral is the Cathedral of the Twelve Apostles and the former patriarch's palace, now a museum. The Russian Church had become independent of its Greek parent in 1589 when the patriarchate was established. Patriarch Filaret, father of the first Romanov ruler, after being captured by the Poles during the Time of Troubles, returned to work closely with his son, the young Tsar Michael (Mikhail). The close relationship between tsar and patriarch continued with the next ruler, Alexis (Alexei), who in 1652 appointed the young and ambitious Nikon as patriarch. For a time Nikon even shared the title of Great Sovereign with the Tsar, and he built in the Kremlin the grand Krestovaya or Cross Hall (1656), more magnificent even than the Tsar's. Patriarch Nikon boldly embarked on a policy of reforming the Russian Church, for so many centuries cut off from the rest of Orthodoxy, and invited leading prelates from the Greek Church to Moscow to help bring Russian practice into line. The results were catastrophic for the social fabric of old Muscovy. The apparently trivial reforms, which included

*17. The house granted by Ivan the Terrible to English merchants of the Muscovy Company on their arrival in Russia in 1553.*

*18. Memorials to the hero-cities of the Second World War line the Kremlin wall to the corner Arsenal Tower.*

making the sign of the cross with three fingers instead of two and a change in the spelling of Jesus' name, were too much for the largely illiterate populace, for whom the outward forms of worship were all-important. Martyrs were burnt at the stake and some monasteries, including the remote Solovetsky, held out for years against the innovations. This stubborn opposition led to the emergence of the Old Believers as a separate sect which to this day does not accept the reforms. In the end, this intransigence caused Nikon's downfall, for the Tsar felt obliged to disown him.

**First Theatre**  If one enters by the Trinity Gate and looks quickly to the right, there is a small street, well-guarded by soldiers. Half-way down it stands a building with an overhanging upper floor, in the manner of old English half-timbered houses. This is the only remaining seventeenth-century house or *palata* of a boyar family in the Kremlin. It once belonged to the Miloslavskys, who fell from power when Mary Miloslavsky, first wife of Tsar Alexis, died and he married Natalia Naryshkin, Peter the Great's mother. Confiscated by the Tsar, the house became the first theatre in Russia, the 'Poteshny' or amusement theatre. In 1918 it was used to house leading Bolsheviks and Stalin and his family lived here until the 1930s. It was here that Nadezhda Alliluyeva, Stalin's wife, shot herself in 1932.

**Arsenal**  The only building erected in the time of Peter the Great in the Kremlin is, appropriately enough, the Arsenal, as Russia was at war virtually throughout his reign. Located on the left as one enters from the

*19. The Armoury Tower (1495), with the Commandant Tower in the background, facing Alexandrov Gardens.*

Trinity Gate, it is a large, two-storey building in the form of a trapezoid to fit the acute angle of the Kremlin walls. Rebuilt after the 1812 fire by Bove, its exterior was modified but the hugely thick walls and paired windows are from the original building and Peter's monogram can still be seen on the interior gateway. Ranged along the front are some of the 800 cannon captured from Napoleon's army in 1812. Now the office of the Kremlin Guard, it is closed to visitors.

**Senate**  Situated next to the Arsenal is the impressive building of the Moscow branch of the former Senate, an institution founded by Peter the Great, built 1787 by Moscow's leading classical architect, Matvei Kazakov. With its long façade punctuated by grand portals, the building forms a rough triangle, over one end of which rests a broad shallow dome on which the Russian flag flies. Kazakov was the most prolific classical architect of the late eighteenth century and the Senate is one of his most remarkable buildings. It contains a fine room, known as the Catherine Hall, where special presentations, such as the award of the former Lenin

*20. Beneath the walls of the Kremlin, a procession of Hari Krishna devotees is a surprising spectacle, indicative of the changed attitude to religion in post-Soviet Russia.*

prizes, are held. Used for the Circuit Court in the nineteenth century, it has since 1918 provided the seat of government or Council of Ministers building where Lenin, Stalin and the other leaders had their offices. In 1955 Lenin's rooms (used by Stalin after Lenin's death), where he had his office and where he and his wife lived, were restored as they were in his lifetime; they used to be occasionally shown to high-ranking delegations.

**Great Kremlin Palace and Armoury Museum** The Great Kremlin Palace, which faces the Moskva River near Cathedral Square, was built (1838-49) under Nicholas I by his favourite architect, Konstantin Ton, in a conspicuous neo-Russian, neo-Byzantine style. Although not the most beautiful building of the Kremlin, its interiors are very lavishly furnished and there are four great halls called after the four senior Russian military orders. The luxurious state rooms seem untouched, as if the dust covers have been left on all these years. In the Thirties, Stalin had two of the grand halls, the Andrew and Alexander, remodelled to provide an assembly hall for the 17th Party Congress. In

the process, the oldest church in the Kremlin, the Saviour in the Wood (1330), which stood in a courtyard was demolished. Two formal halls remain, the impressive St George, which serves as a lobby for delegates, and the Vladimir Hall, where treaties are signed.

At one end of the palace are the courtyard, staircase and chambers of the old Terem Palace, completely hidden within the walls of the later building.

Ton was also the architect of the Armoury Museum, entered from the south-west, Borovitsky Gate. This houses astonishing collections of carriages, royal costumes, crowns, thrones, vessels and other precious artefacts. Among the more unexpected items is the unique collection of Elizabethan and Stuart silver plate, presented to the tsars as gifts from English monarchs, which thus escaped being melted down under Cromwell in the seventeenth century. Perhaps the most popular item is the wonderful collection of royal Faberge Easter eggs which Nicholas II

*22. Religious scenes are often painted over the main portal of Russian churches. This magnificent Virgin and Child was executed in the 1660s at the entrance to the Assumption Cathedral, the pre-eminent church of Russia.*

and Alexander III presented to their wives.

**Supreme Soviet Building** Between the Senate and the Saviour Gate is an ochre, classical building which resembles Moscow's eighteenth-century mansions. In fact, it was built in 1934 as a military school for the Red Commanders. In 1938 it became the seat of the Presidium of the Supreme Soviet, and now houses Russian government offices. It was built on the ruins of the ancient Ascension Convent, which held the tombs of the royal tsaritsas and princesses, and of the famous Monastery of the Miracles, where the monks wrote chronicles and Patriarch Hermogenes starved to death in 1612 during the Polish occupation. The monasteries were demolished in the early Thirties, together with the delightful Nikolaev Palace, where Alexander II was born during a family visit to Moscow. Thus, the comparatively spacious grounds on the east side of the Kremlin were once crowded with buildings. On the brow of the hill a huge monument to Alexander III was erected by the last tsar and pulled down after the Revolution.

23. Eleven cupolas on tall, tiled drums are cunningly linked in three sets of five to serve the many chapels within the ancient Terem Palace, hidden within the walls of the Great Kremlin Palace.

**Palace of Congresses** On the right of the Trinity Gate is the only truly modern building in the Kremlin, the Palace of Congresses. It was erected in 1961 under Khrushchev in the international modern glass-and-concrete style to provide a larger meeting hall for the periodic party congresses. Several floors were built underground to ensure that it did not dominate the other Kremlin buildings. In between congresses it served as a second opera and ballet theatre for the Bolshoi Company. Communist party congresses are no more, but it is equally suitable as premises for other meetings, such as those held by well-known American evangelists.

**Social Life** In the sixteenth and seventeenth centuries, the Kremlin was a hive of activity. Not only did it house the royal family and the senior religious leaders, the principal churches of the land and the offices of government, but the leading boyars too — the Godunovs, Trubetskois, Morozovs — liked to have their homes in the fortified citadel. Once the capital moved to St Petersburg , this crowded population diminished and the streets of the fortress fell silent, only enlivened by the infrequent visits of the reigning monarch — the Empress Anna stayed for two years in Moscow at the commencement of her reign in 1730 — and by the coronation ceremony, which always took place in the Assumption Cathedral. Napoleon also left his mark; he lived for several days in the old Kremlin palaces in 1812 until the great fire drove him north to the safer Peter Palace. It was not until the arrival of the new Soviet government in 1918 that the Kremlin became a lively place again. Many families of the leaders took up residence there, together with others with Soviet connections, like the poet Demyan Bedny. This sociable communal life was stifled when Stalin took control, and by the second half of the Thirties few families remained. (Lenin's wife and sister were almost incarcerated in their Kremlin flat, requiring permission to come and go.) However, the Kremlin has remained at the centre of political life in the Soviet Union/Russia. In 1955, after the death of Stalin, it was opened to visitors for the first time since the Revolution. Those working in the government rubbed shoulders with sightseers. When President Reagan visited in 1988, he was able to come out of the Grand Kremlin Palace, where he was talking with President Gorbachev, to greet tourists in Cathedral Square. Recently the Kremlin has also been reinstated as the religious centre of the Orthodox Church.

# MEDIEVAL SPLENDOUR

Russia's medieval period lasted until the reforms of Peter the Great were introduced in the early 1700s. By the fifteenth century, Moscow had consolidated its hegemony over most of the other Russian cities and in the course of the next two hundred years was even able to extend its influence over independent Novgorod and faraway Pskov. This was the result of several factors. First, Moscow's geographic position at the centre of the north-south, east-west river systems played a crucial role. Second, the city's rulers had ingratiated and enriched themselves as ignominious tax-gatherers for the khans of the Golden Horde; as the Tartar menace declined, Moscow's rulers were able to throw off their increasingly odious control. Third, the Orthodox Church consecrated Moscow's supremacy when Metropolitan Peter moved from Vladimir to Moscow in 1328. But this supremacy was threatened by conflict among the ruling princes of Moscow at the beginning of the fifteenth century that was not

24. The Great Kremlin Palace was built in eclectic style in 1849 by Konstantin Ton as the imperial residence, although it was rarely visited by the tsars.

resolved until the reign of Ivan III in 1462.

The politically important marriage of Ivan III to a princess of Byzantium and the magnificent rebuilding of the Kremlin would seem to have put Muscovy, after years of isolation under the Tartars, firmly on the road to alignment with Europe. But this was not to be. The long reign (1533-84) of the paranoid Ivan the Terrible and widespread illiteracy and suspicion of foreigners inhibited rapid progress in this direction. Enemies abounded: on the west the Lithuanian-Polish state and on the east the Tartars. The end of the Rurikid dynasty at the death of Ivan the Terrible's son, Fyodor, together with a severe famine, led to the Time of Troubles early in the seventeenth century and the invasion and occupation of Moscow by Polish forces (1610-12). Even the establishment in 1613 of a new dynasty, the Romanovs, which provided the three tsars of the century, Michael, Alexis and Peter, was not the end of the troubles. Serious uprisings occurred against the salt tax in 1648, against the debasement of the currency in 1662, and by the very defenders of the state, the Musketeers (Streltsy), at the end of the century. Yet during these two centuries the arts of painting and architecture, little influenced by developments abroad, attained new heights, perhaps never to be equalled. Moscow's most brilliant architects of this period are nearly all unknown, but the fruits of their invention endure.

## KITAI-GOROD

As the city grew and the Kremlin could no longer provide shelter during the dreaded Tartar raids, the eastern district, a rough rectangle enclosing the long established Great Settlement, was surrounded by wide, relatively low walls, built (1534-38) by yet another Italian, Petrok Maly. Kitai-gorod, as it was known, is a name of obscure origin: *kitai* possibly meaning city (but not Chinatown, as it would in modern Russian), or else the wattle used to strengthen the walls. It included the market-place that had grown up on the east side of the Kremlin that was later known as Red or Beautiful Square.

The great walls which had survived virtually intact into the twentieth century and which in some places were so wide that a coach and four could drive along them were dismantled in the 1930s, ostensibly in connection with the construction of the metro. Fortunately, some remnants behind the Metropole Hotel survive, but the section by the Rossiya Hotel was newly built in the 1970s.

In the second half of the nineteenth century up to the Revolution, Kitai-gorod became the financial and trading centre of the Empire and experienced an unprecedented building boom. The new banks, trading houses, warehouses and the Stock Exchange overwhelm the survivals of the medieval period when Kitai-gorod was a haven for influential merchants, forbidden the more prestigious Kremlin, and for foreigners.

The **Church of St Anne** (*Zachatiya Anny 'shto v uglu'*), built in the second half of the fifteenth century with later additions, is situated where the Kitai-gorod walls once turned at right angles back towards the Kremlin, hence its name. Although massively rebuilt after the disastrous fire of 1547, it still exhibits the traditional triple-bayed and gabled wall girdled by a fine frieze. There is a legend that Ivan III married his Byzantine princess, Sophia, in this church as the prelates in the Kremlin

refused to officiate at the wedding of the Grand Prince to a bride associated with the Catholic Pope.

One of Kitai-gorod's three main streets, the Varvarka (until 1987 Razina), played an important role in the sixteenth-century history of Moscow. Along this charming street of churches, now in the shadow of the huge Rossiya Hotel, are two medieval palaces. The white house with the steeply pitched wooden roof set below the street is the **Old English Embassy** (*Stary Angliisky Dvor*), discovered and restored in the 1970s. The English adventurers, led by Richard Chancellor, who in 1553 had chanced upon Muscovy during their quest for a trade route to China, stayed here. Ivan the Terrible received them cordially and with curiosity; later he was intrigued to discover that England was ruled by a queen, Elizabeth, and conceived the idea of marrying her, or at least one of her ladies-in-waiting — a prospect they found decidedly unattractive. Most importantly, the Tsar granted the Muscovy Company a monopoly of trade greatly beneficial to both sides (English ships were then constructed of good Russian timber) that lasted for nearly a century, curtailed only when the head of Charles I was struck off — Russian tsars could not condone regicide. The old white house or *palata* has walls a metre thick and few windows. Under the English merchants, the loft and basement were used for storage and the large rooms on the middle floor for receiving customers and as offices.

Almost next to the Old English Embassy there is another ancient stone *palata*, the former **Romanov House**. In the sixteenth century this was the home of the boyar Nikita Romanov and his family — his sister, Anastasia, was the first and dearest wife of Ivan the Terrible. But after her death, when the Tsar became paranoid, the Romanovs, too, were threatened and were obliged to seek refuge with their good neighbours, the English, on more than one occasion. The English merchants also taught Greek and Latin to the Romanov children, including Michael (Mikhail), the future founder of the Romanov dynasty. The house, which faces the Varvarka, with its checkerboard pattern was built at different times; the high stone basement is certainly original, the ground and first floors probably date from the 1600s, but the wooden upper floor was added in the mid-nineteenth century when, under Alexander II, the house was restored as the birthplace of the Romanovs. In the Soviet period it remained a museum with the more discreet title of Museum of a Boyar's Domestic Life; recently it has again become the Romanov House.

## MONASTERIES AND EXPANSION

Monasteries have always played a prominent role in Russian history. Except for the hermitages, they were not exclusive and served the public not only in spiritual ways but as educational and medical centres and in caring for the poor. In the fourteenth century the number of monasteries increased dramatically and in time they became large landowners on a par with the grand princes. It was not until the late eighteenth century, under Catherine II, that most of their huge estates with their two million serfs were confiscated and about half of all the monasteries were closed. However, over a thousand were still functioning before the Revolution. In the Soviet period, less than a dozen were allowed to continue, and many were physically destroyed.

Within the boundaries of Moscow there were 25 monasteries and

*27. New Maidens (Novodevichy) Convent was a convenient place for confining troublesome female relatives, such as Evdokia, Peter the Great's first wife, or Sofia, his sister and former regent.*

*28. A corner town of New Maidens Convent.*

*30. Minin and Pozharsky, the butcher and the boyar, were the leaders of the army that expelled the Polish invaders in 1612. Their statue by St Basil's, depicting them in antique dress, is by Ivan Martos (1818).*

*29. St Basil's Cathedral, completed in 1561, is the quintessential Russian church. Its architecture, derived from the early wooden churches of the north, was directly influenced by the tower of the Ascension Church at Kolomenskoe and the decoration of the Church of St John the Baptist at Dyakovo, both within the boundaries of present-day Moscow.*

convents before 1917. In 1980 none was functioning, but the buildings and walls of 18 still existed in one form or another. With the revival of the Orthodox Church in the late 1980s, many have reverted to their original, religious use. All have interesting histories and architecture; they were the recipients of much royal attention and some were important centres of religious movements. A group of these monastery-convents even acted as fortresses, strategically placed around Moscow at its most vulnerable points: the west and south threatened by the Polish-Lithuanian empire, and the east liable to attack from the Tartars. Sometimes their black-gowned monks were even obliged to take up arms.

The **New Saviour** (*Novospassky*), moved east from the Kremlin to the banks of the Moskva River in the second half of the fifteenth century, became the burial place of the powerful Romanov boyars and later of the prominent Sheremetiev family. The **Simonov**, a kilometre east of the New Saviour, was a famous religious centre and powerful fortress as it was in the front line of Tartar invasions. Six of its ancient churches were blown up in 1930, leaving only the refectory and three of the tent-shaped towers. The **Danilov**, the oldest foundation, was also the first to be reopened; from 1932 on it had been used as a prison for young offenders. It was beautifully restored and reconsecrated in time for the 1988 millennium of the establishment of Christianity in Russia. The **Donskoi**, founded in 1591 south of the Kremlin, is the newest of the monasteries. It was raised on the site of a victory over the Tartars said to have been due to the miraculous power of the icon of the Virgin of the Don. Its buildings survive, the old and new cathedrals ranking among the most picturesque in Moscow. During the plague of 1771, Archbishop Ambrose, who had enraged the crowd when he forbade the kissing of the icon at the Varvara Gate for fear of spreading the disease, was chased to this monastery,

31. Although wooden carving was not as common as icons in Russian Orthodox churches, in northern Russia there was a tradition of carved religious figures like this pensive St Paraskeva.

where he tried to hide behind the new cathedral altar, but was dragged out and torn limb from limb. The monastery is now an oasis of quiet in the noisy city, especially the old graveyard established in the seventeenth century for aristocrats and the intelligentsia.

The **New Maidens** (*Novodevichy*) **Convent** is the most stunningly beautiful of all Moscow's lovely monasteries. It, too, is situated on the Moskva River facing south, the final link in the chain of fortress-monasteries. Of all of them, it has had the most sensational political history. It

*32. The south portal of the Cathedral of the Saviour of Andronikov Monastery displays the receding pointed arches and bulbous melons on the columns typical of early Moscow architecture. Built in 1427, it is the oldest building in the city.*

was founded in 1524 to commemorate the taking of Smolensk from the Poles (who recaptured it a few decades later; it was not until the middle of the seventeenth century that Smolensk definitively joined Russia). It is named after the Smolensk icon, the miracle-working Virgin Hodegetriya (mother and child *en face*). The convent, with close connections to the imperial family, is conveniently located at the end of Prechistenka, a straight road that leads directly to the Kremlin's Borovitsky Gate.

In the famous scene in Pushkin's *Boris Godunov* and Mussorgsky's

*33. This late 17th-century pala-ta, once the home of a rich merchant, is one of about 30 houses of this period that have survived in Moscow. The niche at the centre of the house was under a grand porch used on formal occasions to greet important visitors.*

*34. The beautiful tower churches began with the wooden churches of the north. The Ascension, at the royal estate at Kolomenskoe, built in 1532 in honour of the birth of Ivan the Terrible, is the first expression in stone of this style and influenced the design of St Basil's.*

opera, the tsar-elect comes to the convent to await the call to the throne; his sister, the consort of the deceased Tsar Fyodor for whom Godunov had acted as regent, was buried in the convent.

During the Time of Troubles and Polish intervention, the convent was badly damaged and was rebuilt only in the 1680s during the reign, again as regent, of Sophia, Peter the Great's sister. In 1689 Peter took the throne from his unwilling half-sister and obliged her to retire to this convent. Sophia lived in some style until the second Musketeer (Streltsy) uprising in her name in 1698. Peter, having just returned from his tour of western Europe, quelled the insurgents with unspeakable cruelty and this time forced Sophia to take the veil, incarcerating her in the convent she had done so much to beautify. On his orders, the bodies of some of the slain Streltsy were hung outside the window of her chambers by the south gate, where they dangled all winter.

Sophia, who took the name of Susannah when she became a nun, lies in the **Novodevichy Cathedral**, along with two of her sisters. Peter also used the convent to get rid of his first wife, Evdokia, whom he married when he was only seventeen to please his mother. Her tomb is also in the cathedral.

The cathedral, positioned in the centre of the roughly walled square that encloses the convent, is a large building in the form of an elongated cube with a gallery on three sides. Although constructed fifty years afterwards, its design is based on the Assumption Cathedral in the Kremlin. The interior has some of the finest sixteenth-century frescoes in Moscow on the vaulting; others were done in the second half of the seventeenth century. The remarkable iconostasis of carved wood, its columns in the

*35. The Church of the Kazan Virgin at Kolomenskoe (1650) is typical of the patterned churches of the mid-17th century with its elaborate window frames, its gallery, now enclosed, and its peaked porch. It was the chapel of the fabulous wooden palace of Tsar Alexis, to which it was connected by passageways.*

*36. The new bell and belfry are indications of the renewal of Moscow's churches, nowhere more evident than here at the restored Nativity Church 'v Starom Simonove' within the precincts of a big factory.*

*37. The colourful gate to the Yusupovs' 17th-century palata was added in the late 19th century, when the house was heavily restored and redecorated. The Yusupov crest is on the gateway.*

form of grape vines, was completed in 1685.

Nearly all the other churches, the elegant bell tower and walls were erected during the reconstruction of the 1680s, thus displaying a single architectural style — the richly decorated red and white Moscow (Naryshkin) baroque. Even the walls with their merlons, the towers with lacy finishes, and the tall, elegant bell tower contribute to this harmony. The two gate churches are particularly splendid. At the north entrance the **Church of the Transfiguration** (*Preobrazheniya*) welcomes the faithful with its tall drums, its elegant, elongated, gold cupolas, and its shell window designs like those of the Archangel Cathedral in the Kremlin. At the south, the **Church of the Intercession** is divided into three great arches, each with its own tall slender drum on an octagonal base topped by a gold cupola. The long low refectory (*trapeznaya*) **Church of the Assumption** also dates from this short building period.

The Novodevichy Convent, which was one of the richest and most powerful in Muscovy, was deprived of its extensive lands by the edict of 1762 and after that suffered a slow decline. It still remained an important religious house, as the nineteenth-century graves scattered in its grounds indicate. There were originally more than two thousand of these graves within the grounds, but in the 1930s most of them were desecrated to provide marble for the building of the metro. Fortunately, Anton Chekhov's grave was transferred to the old cemetery just beyond the south wall of the convent. Other graves that have survived include those of the Decembrists Matvei Muraviev-Apostol and Sergei Trubetskoi, the historians Sergei Soloviev and Mikhail Pogodin, and the adventurer-poet Denis Davydov.

**City Walls**  City fortifications continued to be constructed in an increasingly wide radius from the Kremlin. Following the devastating raid in 1571 by the Crimean khan, Devlit-Girei, wide stone walls were erected in place of earthen ramparts encircling the district known as Bely Gorod (white city) — 'white' denoting exemption from tax for those who lived there. The walls, four to five metres thick and nine kilometres in circumference, were built in 1586-93 under the direction of Fyodor Kon. By the eighteenth century they were seriously dilapidated and were gradually replaced by the pleasant tree-lined boulevards that now circle old Moscow, providing green spaces for areas without gardens.

Moscow's second defensive ring, now the Garden (Sadovaya) Ring Road, was not built of stone or brick but consisted of earthen ramparts with wooden palisading. Sixteen kilometres around, it crossed the river to include the hitherto unprotected Zamoskvoreche quarter. Although the walls soon lost any military significance and proved no obstacle to the invasions of the Poles in 1610 or the French in 1812, they bequeathed to the city its attractive radial/circular street plan. The Garden Ring Road was so named because in the 18th-19th centuries front gardens to every property extended almost to the middle of the road, leaving only a narrow channel for traffic. Stalin removed these green oases in 1937 to make way for the existing monstrous twelve- to fourteen-lane highway.

**Inner Monasteries**  The monasteries within the city — Sretenka (The Meeting), Rozhdestvensky, (Nativity), Vysoko Petrovsky, Chudov (Miracle), Ivanov — were less vulnerable to attack and became educational or charitable institutions. The white-limestone **Cathedral of the Nativity** (*Rozhdestvensky*) at the convent of the same name on the

Boulevard dates from the beginning of the sixteenth century, and is one of the oldest surviving buildings in the city. With its three round apses extruding boldly from the square of the structure and the pointed gables climbing one over the other to the drum of the helmet-shaped cupola, its pleasing architecture is a happy mixture of round forms and right angles, the whole giving a triangular, pyramidal effect, a much-loved Russian form. Not long after the cathedral was built, Vasily, the reigning grand prince, determined to divorce his barren wife, Simonia, and marry another to ensure an heir to the throne. Simonia put up a spirited resistance but eventually, in 1525, she was forced to become a nun in the Nativity Convent. When Vasily married Yelena Glinskaya, soon to be mother to the future Ivan the Terrible, Simonia was sent, still protesting, to the Pokrov Convent in Suzdal, east of Moscow, where rumours abounded that she had given birth to a son, Georgy. In 1934 the graves were opened and her secret was revealed: near her tomb, wrapped in fine cloth and adorned with jewels, was a doll.

**The Andronikov**  In the eastern part of the city, on the banks of the Yauza near the confluence with the Moskva, the Andronikov Monastery was founded on the route to the then important city of Vladimir. The greatest icon painter in Russia, Andrei Rublev, worked and died there, although sadly none of his frescoes survive in the monastery. At its centre is the oldest and perhaps most beautiful building in Moscow, the **Cathedral of the Saviour** (*Spassky Sobor*, 1427), triple-bayed and triple-apsed, with pointed gables clustering around the single, helmet-shaped cupola. Damaged in the 1812 fire, it had been much altered, but in the 1930s Soviet restorers set about researching and restoring the church, a task that took them nearly thirty years. The result is a magnificent testimony to their tenacity and skill. In Tolstoy's time, traffic was heavy as weary prisoners trudged past on their way to the notorious prisons in Vladimir and Siberia. At the end of the nineteenth century, the district was built up with large factories which, although run-down, are still functioning. Yet the white-walled monastery by the river remains an oasis of calm, oblivious to the clatter of machinery and trams. Closed after the Revolution, it then became a notorious prison controlled by the secret police. In 1947 the Andrei Rublev Icon Museum was opened there, and nowadays the cathedral, sometimes used as a concert hall, is functioning again as a church.

**Early Parish Churches**  The **Church of St Nikita** (*Nikitiy 'shto za Yauzy'*), also on Moscow's eastern side, was built somewhat later, at the end of the sixteenth century, but on the crypt of an earlier church. With its seventeenth-century chapel and bell tower, it is one of the most picturesque buildings in Moscow. The older part bears a helmet-shaped cupola and round gables, whereas the later chapel supports an onion cupola and peaked gables. Closed in the Thirties, it suffered in the godless years under Stalin; it was described as a heap of ruins in 1948 in Solzhenitsyn's *First Circle*. Carefully restored (1958-60), its buildings were then taken over by Diafilm, manufacturers of photographic slides. However, with the new freedom of religious practice, St Nikita, too, has returned to the Church. Sadly, the remarkable view of the Kremlin once enjoyed by the church is now totally hidden by the Stalin-era high-rise Gothic tower block that stands at the confluence of the Yauza and the Moskva.

There are a few other stone churches of these early times in Moscow, some situated far from the centre. One such is the **Church of St**

**Trifon** (*'v Naprudnom'*), north of the Garden Ring, built in the late fifteenth-early sixteenth century. Here bricks, which had only just begun to be used, were employed sparingly for details — the cornices, drum of the cupola and the curious old-fashioned bell tower standing on the roof like a tocsin. This charming little church, open for worship once more, with its distinctive cupola and rare bell tower (it soon became the custom in Moscow for bell towers to be separate or attached to the western end of churches) is now swamped by tower blocks erected in the Seventies.

Another of Moscow's earliest churches, located even further from the centre, is perhaps its most odd. It is the **Church of the Nativity** (*Rozhdestva 'v Starom Simonove'*), built in the early sixteenth century on the banks of the Moskva several kilometres east of the Kremlin. It became a particularly cherished church when the two priests who accompanied Dmitry Donskoi to the Battle of Kulikovo in 1380, Peresvet and Oslyabya, were reburied there. In the nineteenth century this part of Moscow became a factory district and the church found itself, in 1897, on the edge of the territory of Dinamo, a Belgian firm manufacturing electric motors. After the Revolution, Dinamo expanded, becoming one of the largest factories in Moscow, and swallowed up the old church, which it used to house heavy compressors. In the early 1980s, the Society for the Protection of Monuments, after long and difficult negotiations, obtained the factory's agreement to remove the compressors and allow restoration of the church. This still did not solve the problem of access, for the factory was most reluctant to allow the public onto its territory. An ingenious solution was found: a long, enclosed passageway was built to the church from the small park bordering the factory. Visitors enter the dark recesses of the passageway and emerge into the light to see, framed in the mouth of the tunnel, the beautiful whitewashed church. Religious services are now taking place in this most secretive and rewarding of Moscow's old buildings, and the two saints have been commemorated again.

## PALACES

Secular buildings in the sixteenth and seventeenth centuries were usually built of wood, which was not only easily obtainable but regarded as warmer than stone in the cold winters. Even the most eminent boyars and grand princes built the upper parts of their houses of wood, although the ground-floor level might be of stone. So it was a new development when stone *palata* or mansions began to appear in Moscow. Some thirty houses from this period have survived, scattered throughout the city, built for wealthy individuals or for the more successful craft settlements, the medieval guilds.

The **Troekurov Palace**, painted a joyous red and white, is tucked behind and almost hidden by the tall Gosplan building, a Soviet building of the Thirties now used by the Russian government. Troekurov was an important boyar, head of the *Streltsy* — the Musketeers of Moscow — who acted as Guards regiments before a regular army was established. Of the three floors, the basement is the oldest and simplest, the ground floor has the distinctive peaked window frames common in the first half of the seventeenth century, and the first floor, built fifty years later, has the more elaborate window designs of the early baroque period.

Near the Armenian settlement in Sverchkov Lane stands a splendid

old house on two floors with a deep basement. The main section of the **Sverchkov Palace** was built for the wealthy merchant Sverchkov in a series of linked rooms. The upper living floor, originally of wood, was rebuilt in 1660 of brick, with porches and an outer gallery that have not survived. Sverchkov, who not only resided here but ran his business from this building, was the main donor to the tall Church of the Assumption (1699) that stood near his house. Napoleon called it the most beautiful church in the city but, tragically, it fell victim to the bulldozers of the Thirties.

Yet the most dramatically beautiful of Moscow's early houses must surely be the grand **Yusupov Palace** (now offices for the Academy of Agriculture), built in the late seventeenth century. Its first and second owners, the diplomat Shafirov and boyar Volkov, fell in the struggle for power waged by Peter the Great's closest advisor, Menshikov, after the Tsar's death. In 1727 the picturesque house passed to Grigory Yusupov, whose powerful family held the property for nearly two hundred years, until the Revolution of 1917.

Here, all the motifs of medieval Russia can be found — colour in the red walls with white stone detailing, massed windows with their elaborately designed frames, pendules, porches, a checkerboard roof, and the charming lack of symmetry. Its interior, repainted in the nineteenth century in an attempt to mimic its earlier decor, is ostentatiously florid.

## TOWER CHURCHES

No matter how one prepares oneself, the first glimpse of the **Cathedral of the Intercession of the Virgin** (*Sobor Pokrova*), more

*40. The entranceway opens into the tall main body of the church, rising upwards to the cupola. The iconostasis, the tall screen in front of the altar, displays the icons arranged in an established order. Those of Christ in Majesty flanked by the Virgin and John the Baptist are the largest and most splendid.*

popularly known as **St Basil's**, is nothing less than astonishing. This bizarre conglomeration of colour, form and texture seems to defy definition. Yet its *raison d'être* can be discerned and its architectural motifs clearly understood from earlier models. Its patron was Ivan the Terrible, the tsar who dominated the sixteenth century.

Ivan came to the throne in 1533 at the age of three. He spent his childhood among aggressive boyars who pushed the boy aside in their lust for power. When he was crowned in 1547 at the age of seventeen, a devastating fire broke out which ravaged the entire city. And when his beloved wife, Anastasia, died in 1560, Ivan thought she had been poisoned. All these events combined to turn him into a deeply suspicious and cruel despot. Yet there were some positive features to Ivan's long reign. He expanded the boundaries of Russia by moving into Siberia, opened contacts with the West through his relations with English merchants, brought in the first printing press, and continued the push against the Tartars. The young Tsar and his army were the victors in a famous battle in 1552 against the Volga Tartars, entrenched in the city of Kazan some five hundred miles east of Moscow. To commemorate the event, the Tsar decided to built a great church not in the Kremlin, as his forbears would have done, but in Red Square, the market-place and lively centre of the now populous city of some one hundred thousand people. St Basil's was the result.

The victory occurred on the feast of the Intercession of the Virgin, the *Pokrova*, after which the new cathedral was named. As it took eight attempts to conquer Kazan, the Tsar decreed that the church should be constructed with eight chapels, seven grouped around a central altar. However, for purposes of symmetry, the architect (or architects) built eight chapels with alternating high and low textured cupolas ringed around the central ninth and united by an open gallery. The central core of the church was to be a long slender pyramidal tower punctuated with windows and ending in a small cupola. Octagonal shapes, round arches and acute gables dominate the design of the church. In the seventeenth century its picturesqueness was enhanced when it was painted in many colours. The revered holy fool Vasily (Basil) was buried in the walls of the cathedral shortly after it was built, hence its more popular name. St Basil's was the scene of the Palm Sunday service, when the patriarch on a horse (simulating an ass) was led by the tsar from the Kremlin through Spassky Gate to the cathedral. After the Revolution, St Basil's was closed and turned into a museum. But in April 1992 it again resounded to the great Easter service.

The origins of St Basil's are to be found in two churches in the Moscow suburbs. In 1532 the royal estate at Kolomenskoe on the banks of the Moskva River, some ten kilometres south-east of the Kremlin, was enhanced by a splendid tower church built by Vasily III in honour of the birth of his son Ivan, later the Terrible. The tall **Church of the Ascension** (*Vozneseniya*), surrounded on three sides by an open gallery, rises via three rows of sharply pointed gables to an octagon, from which the tower narrows to the small cupola that defines its summit. The style is a clear derivation from wooden tower churches, an indigenous Russian architectural form, which arose in the north and was first translated into stone in this beautiful building. The central tower of St Basil's is clearly influenced by this church.

Across the ravine, only half a kilometre away, is a second stone church built at almost the same time. **St John the Baptist** (*Ioann Predtechi*) was erected about 1547 to celebrate the birth of the son of Ivan the Terrible, or perhaps in honour of Ivan's coronation. It is not a tower church but incorporates many of the details found in St Basil's, such as round and sharp arrow-like gables one above the other. Its plan, too, of four chapels around a central octagon influenced that of the cathedral.

Although rare, there are other tower churches in Moscow. In 1640 in the northern part of the city on the banks of the Yauza River at Medvedkovo, the **Church of the Intercession** was built by Prince Pozharsky (the hero who with Kuzma Minin had expelled the Poles from Moscow, after a two-year occupation, in 1612, thus signifying the end of the Time of Troubles). Intended as a memorial to the liberation of Russia, the church consciously mimics features of St Basil's of a century earlier. The elegant tower decorated with ceramic diamonds rises above the basic cube. It is surrounded on three sides by a gallery, once open but now enclosed, and flanked by chapels, each with its own cupola.

The last church to be built in this style is the **Nativity of Our Lady** (*Rozhdestva 'v Putinkakh'*) just north of Pushkin Square. It was near the palace where foreign travellers could freshen up after their long journey to Moscow. It is richly endowed with five towers in all: three over the central cube, another over a side chapel, and yet another as bell tower. The whole mass is linked by the low form of the entrance (*trapeznaya*), which has a particularly fine doorway with its own octagonal tower. This church, actually paid for by Tsar Alexis, was to be the last of the tower churches. The powerful Patriarch Nikon, who introduced many controversial reforms in church ritual and architecture, decreed in 1652 that

there should be no more tower churches, that churches 'should have five cupolas and not resemble a tent...' However, the tent-shaped tower was so beloved of Russian builders that it tended to creep back under disguised forms.

## SCHISM AND COLOUR

Patriarch Nikon's reforms resulted in the most serious division ever to occur in the Russian Orthodox Church, the splitting away of the traditionalist Old Believers, a schism not healed to this day. In the still predominantly wooden city, he favoured the stone and brick churches which, with their asymmetrical design — the linkage of separate chambers and differing roof levels, the use of decorative individual window frames and love of bright colour — give the city its most distinctive personality. There is a certain joy about these churches. In spite of the civil unrest that plagued the seventeenth century, it was a period of unexampled construction of picturesque stone and brick buildings, so many of which have survived the centuries. Likewise, the art of painting, expressed in icons and frescoes, flourished. By the end of the century, the dynamic Peter the Great was on the throne and the painting of religious subjects started slowly to make way for the secular. The narrow Russian vision then began, painfully yet determinedly, to open out to embrace western Europe.

**Church of the Trinity** The wealthy Yaroslavl merchant Grigory Nikitnikov seems to have deliberately set out to construct an ensemble more magnificent than any of the Kremlin boyars. As a rich merchant and leading member of the guild with wide privileges, including the right to travel, he was nevertheless not permitted to build his home in the Kremlin. The Church of the Trinity (*Troitsy 'v Nikitnikakh'*) in Kitaigorod (1628-51), one of the most colourful in Moscow, was built as his family church alongside his now vanished palace. It is an amazing sight. Its position, next to the pretentious buildings of the former Central Committee of the Communist Party, is most incongruous.

Built on a high crypt used for storing wares — safer from thieves if placed under the altar — its red and white façade is crowded with detail. Everything is here: elaborate and varied window designs, complex cornices, tiers of peaked gables outlined in red and white, the porch with tent-shaped roof and pendules, the elaborate staircase to the entrance. Within, the frescoes executed shortly after the church was built by the last of the great icon artists, Simon Ushakov, are simply magnificent. Closed after the Revolution, damaged by a German bomb in 1941, it is now a well-maintained museum which is resisting attempts to return it to the Church.

**Alekseevskoe** Other splendidly colourful churches of this period include the **Tikhvin Church** in Alekseevskoe in the north of Moscow, next to the modern Cosmos Hotel. This Church of the Tikhvin Icon of the Virgin, built in 1676-82, was part of the royal palace of Tsar Alexis which accommodated him and his numerous court on their pilgrimages to the monastery of Troitse-Sergeyevo (Zagorsk) to the north. The Tsar really used these excursions as an excuse to go hunting, which he loved, so in effect this was a hunting lodge. The palace, which was of wood, has not survived, but the church, a tall cube with a gallery on the crypt, an extruding apse, and tiers of gables supporting the five drums, presents a

*43. A wooden baroque iconostasis in one of the chapels of St Basil's.*

*44. This corner of St Basil's calls to mind Russian wooden toys and the famous lacquer boxes.*

*45. The opulent late 19th-century interior of the Sandunovsky Steam Baths.*

vivid picture with its red background, white detailing and striking blue domes.

**Krutitskoe Podvore** One of the most impressive group of buildings from the seventeenth century is at Krutitskoe Podvore, the grand residence of the most senior churchman after the patriarch, the metropolitan of Krutitskoe and Kolomna. The patriarchate had been finally established in Russia in 1589 and the metropolitan had been obliged to give him his Kremlin residence. Therefore the metropolitan built a new

46. The pyramid shape was
revived in Russia in the late
17th century with Moscow
baroque. The vivid red and
white Trinity Church at Fili
(1694) is an outstanding example of this style. So as not to dis-
turb the symmetry, the bells are
placed in the tower rather than
in a separate building.

palace and churches at a point on the Moskva River where it makes a sharp (*krutoi*) turn, hence the name, and from where, until recently, a magnificent view could be had of the Kremlin.

A colourful ensemble built in the last two decades of the century forms the entrance to the courtyard of the metropolitan's palace. On the left, on a high crypt, is the **Church of the Assumption** (*Uspeniya*), connected by a long gallery to the residence. At the archway into the courtyard, it becomes a steeply roofed house or teremok with four elaborate windows, the whole faced with brightly coloured tiles of green, yellow and brown. Through these windows the metropolitan could admire the view of the Kremlin. However, the property did not remain long in his hands; in 1712 the capital was removed to St Petersburg and in 1721 Peter the Great abolished the patriarchate and Krutitskoe reverted to the crown. It was employed at various times as soldiers' barracks (which are still there) and a prison, but the metropolitan's grand palace now contains a small museum of medieval metalwork. An early, fifteenth-century church in the south part of the complex is under restoration and holding services.

# GUILD SETTLEMENTS

In old Russia, the settlements (*slobody*) were districts specialising in various trades, manufacture, cloth, food preparation, and even gardening. The entire city outside the Kremlin and boyars' palaces consisted of these organised groups of artisans, not unlike medieval guilds, engaged in one particular trade or craft, living together, sometimes behind palisades, and ruled by strict codes of behaviour. The Musketeers (Streltsy) were organised in such settlements in a circle around the edge of the old city.

A particularly rich settlement was that of the weavers in Khamovniki (from *khaman* meaning white cloth), who came from Tver in the early part of the seventeenth century and settled in western Moscow as court weavers. **St Nicholas** (*Nikoly 'v Khamovnikakh'*) was constructed in 1682 as their church. The old building that served as their centre has also survived and is located in the next street. Although the settlement disappeared in the eighteenth century, the area is still dominated by textile manufacture in the form of silk weaving. The church, even including the bell tower, has come down complete, a rarity for Moscow. The whole effect is rather like a ship, a long body crowned at the eastern end by cupolas and at the other, western end, by the mast-like tent-shaped bell tower. The window designs are fantastic, the second tier bearing star-like crowns. But it is the use of colour that is the most striking feature of this splendid church: tiles and trim of red and green in sharp contrast to the white walls and gold cupolas. This church and its interior, rich with nineteenth-century frescoes, was not closed after the Revolution.

Zamoskvoreche ('Across the river') is a most rewarding part of Moscow for the casual visitor; there are still many churches and old houses located within a small area and the southward-flowing streets nearly always give magnificent views of the Kremlin. **St Nicholas** (*Nikoly 'v Pyzhakh'*) was built 1657 as the church of the local Musketeer settlement led by a Captain Pyzhov. The Musketeers, the guardians of the Kremlin, engaged in trade or crafts when not on militia duty. All that is

left of this settlement is this church, with its wonderful, sculptured façade, on which richly decorated window frames encroach on the entablature, and with a roof of three rows of pointed gables topped by five heavy cupolas.

Across from the Kremlin, on the island where the British Embassy is situated, is the unique example of an estate of a leading member of Tsar Alexis' council. It consists of the church and *palata* or mansion (1657) of Averky Kirillov, a *dumny dyak* (member of the council). He was also in charge of the island garden settlement that provided food for the Kremlin. Kirillov's richly patterned **Church of St Nicholas** (*Nikoly 'v Bersenyove'*) is complemented by the stone house, especially its eastern side, once joined to the church by a gallery. The façade of the house was altered in the early years of the eighteenth century with the addition of volutes in the baroque manner, like a Dutch house. These details and the shell-like window pediments of the first floor were daring expressions of the new Petrine Moscow. Kirillov, however, did not live to see it: he was murdered in the bloody Musketeer (Streltsy) uprising of 1682 and is buried near the church.

## MOSCOW [NARYSHKIN] BAROQUE

With the death of Tsar Alexis in 1676 and the reign of his eldest son, the weakling Tsar Fyodor, rivalry broke out between the two families, the Miloslavskys and Naryshkins, who represented the late Tsar's two wives. Peter, only three years old, remained in the background while his elder, Miloslavsky half-brother ruled for six years before dying without issue. The Council then chose the nine-year-old Peter, a Naryshkin, over his feeble-minded elder half-brother, Ivan, a Miloslavsky. At this the Musketeer Guard rioted, broke into the Kremlin, and for three days ran amok murdering many of the Naryshkins and their supporters. Finally, it was agreed that Ivan would be co-tsar with Peter, both under the regency of Peter's half-sister (and a Miloslavsky), Sophia. The pre-eminence of the Miloslavskys, however, lasted only seven years until Peter came of age. Then he gathered support at the Troitse-Sergiev Monastery north of Moscow and took the city without opposition, banishing his sister to the Novodevichy Convent. Thus the Naryshkins finally emerged victorious. In their triumph, they sponsored many new churches and secular buildings in the distinctive Moscow baroque style that became associated with their name.

This new baroque style, which came to Moscow (through the prism of Ukrainian experience) from Italy, expressed itself in a reaffirmation of the old pyramid and octagonal forms so firmly suppressed only fifty years earlier by Patriarch Nikon. Thus, symmetry returned to church architecture. Even the ubiquitous bell tower was dispensed with on the grounds that it disturbed the symmetry of the church; bells were hung in the upper octagonal tier and the churches were known as 'under the bells'.

Happily, several examples of this colourful style survive in Moscow. The huge **Cathedral of the Epiphany** (*Bogoyavleniya*, 1696) in the monastery of that name in Kitai-gorod is an example of this period (it has been under restoration for at least twenty years). One of the oldest monasteries in Moscow, it was closely associated with the Golitsyn family, many of whose graves were removed from the church after the

Revolution and placed in the Donskoi Monastery.

At Troitse-Lykovo in western Moscow across from Serebryanny Bor, the **Church of the Trinity** (*Troitsy*, 1698), built by a member of the Naryshkin family, is an outstanding example of this style. Three octagonal tiers balanced by chapels on either side rise above the cube to meet the gold cupola. It is perfectly balanced, yet intricate and highly ornate, the roofs of each succeeding tier boasting its own sculptured silhouette.

But the best example of Naryshkin baroque is the **Church of the Intercession** (*Pokrova 'v Filyakh'*) in the south-west part of Moscow. It was built in 1693 on the estate of Lev Naryshkin, Peter's uncle and a proponent of the new style. An open gallery surrounds the quatrefoil main summer church over which are three octagonal tiers, the topmost hung with bells. At basement level is the smaller winter church. The geometry and colouring have few equals — circles, ogee shapes, quatrefoil, arches and octagonals, white detailing on red brick, topped by the gold cupola and intricate cross. Happily, its use as a museum and concert hall has preserved the sculpted and rich interiors. Factory chimneys of the nineteenth and twentieth centuries surround the church on all sides, making its unusual beauty the more remarkable. At the time of writing, a struggle is going on between museum and church for use of the building. The museum has blocked off the property, but the small congregation is stubbornly holding services outside in the open air.

# INNOVATIONS OF PETER THE GREAT

At the end of the seventeenth century Peter the Great, the young and extremely energetic tsar, was on the throne. Peter was the first Russian ruler to travel abroad — greatly to the distress of his subjects — and he absorbed much during his stays in Holland and England, becoming convinced of the necessity to modernise Russia on the lines of western Europe. As a child he had witnessed the massacre of his beloved uncles at the hands of the rebelling Musketeers, and on his return from his travels another incipient uprising was quickly quelled. Meanwhile, his courtiers and boyars, obliged to wear European dress and shave their beards, did not welcome the new ways.

Nevertheless, at the beginning of the eighteenth century Moscow began to acquire a new look, one that reflected the changes being introduced by Peter. As he was interested in all things practical, the Tsar was fascinated by the art of construction and before he became engrossed in building his new capital, he and his closest colleagues, many of whom were foreigners, were responsible for introducing a more European appearance in Moscow. Peter wanted to reform his backward people and establish schools, hospitals, theatres, libraries and modern military buildings like the ones he had seen on his travels. Apart from the Arsenal in the Kremlin, most of his secular buildings in Moscow have disappeared, including in Soviet times the great Sukharev Tower in which his mathematical and navigational school was housed. Several churches, however, provide the link between the late seventeenth-century Moscow or Naryshkin style and the western baroque that came in on Peter's coat-tails.

**Monastery of the Saviour** The Monastery of the Saviour 'behind the icon-sellers' (*Zaikonospassky*) is situated in Kitai-gorod, not far from

GUM on Nikolskaya Street. The first institute of higher education in Moscow, the Slavono-Greek-Latin Academy, where many famous scholars studied, including the great polymath Lomonosov, opened in this monastery in 1687. The **Saviour Cathedral** (1709), crowded within the small courtyard, is made up of octagonal tiers on a cube. It bears on each façade a semi-circular pediment at the centre, parapets with balustrades, circular windows and early examples of the use of the classical orders — Vignola's book on the architectural orders was printed several times in Peter's reign.

**Menshikov Tower**  A more dramatic and bold building for the time is the Menshikov Tower or **Church of the Archangel Gabriel** (*Arkhangela Gavriila*). It was built (1705-07) on the estate of Prince Alexander Menshikov, the pieman who rose to become the most powerful man in Russia. The architect, Ivan Zarudny, was a sculptor, and the church reflects this art both inside and out. Hitherto, the Orthodox Church had banned sculpture, but its power weakened under Peter, when it became fashionable to ape European models.

Prince Menshikov set out to build the tallest building in Moscow, higher even than the Kremlin bell tower, with a tall wooden spire and on the summit the figure of the Archangel Gabriel holding the cross. In 1723 lightning destroyed the wooden spire, which came tumbling down, never to be rebuilt so high again. The church is still magnificent, however, with pilasters, volutes, round pediments, columns and capitals, and octagonal tiers surmounted by a gold finial. Menshikov moved to St Petersburg and lost interest in his magnificent Moscow property; after Peter's death in 1725 he fell from power and was banished to Siberia.

Because Prince Menshikov's property was taken over by the new Post Office at the end of the eighteenth century, the Archangel Gabriel became the Post Office church until the Revolution. As the bell tower tier had been lost, St Fyodor Stratilati was erected alongside the Archangel Gabriel in 1806 to act as holder of its bells. Both churches now belong to the patriarchate of Antioch.

**Church of St John the Warrior**  Ivan Zarudny built another church in Moscow, St John the Warrior (*Ioanna Voina*), situated on the Yakimanka on the main road south. It is said that Tsar Peter himself was involved in its construction. He had noticed, while travelling in the spring of 1709, a church entirely surrounded by water and stopped to enquire its name. On hearing John the Warrior, his patron saint, he commanded a new church be built higher up on the street to avoid flooding and sent his own plan forthwith. Thus, under Zarudny's supervision, the church was completed by 1713, just in time to avoid the ban on brick and stone building that enabled all craftsmen and materials to be devoted to St Petersburg.

It is a truly transitional church, bridging the gap between Moscow baroque and the western form. The octagonal tiers and separate octagonal bell tower are still present, but the segmental gables on all four sides, highly decorated architraves, small oval windows, and the volutes of the topmost stage speak of borrowings from western baroque. The building was admired by the leading architect of the late eighteenth century, Vasily Bazhenov. The church, not closed in the Soviet period, was embellished by icons saved from demolished or closed churches, including the icon of the Saviour that hung over the Kremlin Spassky Gate.

*48. State Councillor Averky Kirillov built his house (palata) in the Garden Settlement across the river from the Kremlin in the 1650s. The main façade was altered in the fashionable Dutch style in the early 1700s.*

*49. The exceptional Gothic bridge by Vasily Bazhenov is part of the ambitious palace commissioned by Catherine II for herself and her son at Tsaritsyno in the 1770s, but lack of funds, her displeasure with Bazhenov and with her son meant it was never completed.*

# THE CLASSICAL ERA

At the beginning of the eighteenth century, Moscow was abandoned for the building site that was then St Petersburg. All the master-builders, stone masons, and carpenters were transported to the shores of the Baltic to build the new capital, and in Moscow all new building in brick and stone was forbidden until 1728. The old city in Pushkin's immortal phrase was 'put in the shade by the younger capital like a purple-clad dowager by a new tsaritsa'. In 1737 one of the worst fires in Moscow's history further contributed to its plight. However, one of Peter the Great's new generation of architects, Ivan Mordvinov, whom he had sent abroad to study, chose on his return to work in Moscow instead of St Petersburg. At his death, Ivan Michurin, his assistant, took on the job of restoring the ravaged city, and in the process prepared the first map and further extended its boundaries to the Kamer-Kollezhsky Val, where today's railway stations are situated.

The eighteenth century was a unique period of strong empresses punctuated by short reigns of weak emperors, as the tsars now styled themselves. Moscow's long period of neglect was somewhat alleviated by the lengthy sojourns of the empresses in the old capital. The Empress Anna (1730-40), who was more German than Russian, stayed for two years in Moscow after her coronation. And the Empress Elizabeth (1741-61), the granddaughter of Peter the Great, moved her entire court and government of some 24,000 persons, a quarter of the population of St Petersburg, to Moscow for the elaborate ceremonies surrounding her coronation. Thereafter she often visited the old capital. Elizabeth, with her cheerful and lively nature, stamped her personality on the cities in which she lived by her preference for the lightness and colour of baroque.

## MATURE BAROQUE

In Moscow, European baroque enjoyed a brief fling in the hands of Prince Ukhtomsky, the leading architect of the middle of the eighteenth century, but few of his buildings survive. He founded the first school of architecture in Russia, where many of the leading architects of the second half of the century studied. His exuberant Red Gate (Krasnye Vorota), with its gilded sculpture and rich decor modelled on the arch for the Empress Elizabeth's coronation, was unceremoniously demolished in the 1930s.

Ukhtomsy was probably the author of **St Nikita the Martyr** (*Nikity-Muchenika*, 1751), one of the few examples in Moscow of the Elizabethan period. It is surprising these days to find the noble, red and white St Nikita, with its paired pilasters, large baroque windows, porticoes, broad cupola and spire, in a rundown factory district. Staraya Basmannaya (formerly Karl Marx St) on the east side of Moscow led, in the eighteenth century, to the former Foreigners' Settlement, (*Nemetskaya Sloboda*).

Tsar Alexis in the middle of the seventeenth century confined foreigners to this remote district to avoid the risk of Russians being contaminated by aliens. But his careful segregation of foreigners had the opposite to the desired effect on his young son, the future Peter the Great. As a young boy Peter became fascinated by the orderly, walled village situated on the Yauza River a short way downstream from his mother's palace at Preobrazhenskoe. It made a deep impression on him, and the people he met there became his closest friends. Ironically, the Foreigner's Settlement, rather than discouraging contact with foreigners, was instrumental in turning the young tsar towards the West. The influence of the Foreigner's Settlement continued to grow: a quarter of a century after Peter's death this area of Moscow had become highly fashionable and the

*50. St Nicholas, in one of the small pictures of his life which often surround the main icon portrait, saves the three innocents by warding off the sword thrust.*

main road to it from the centre, one of the most elegant avenues.

Situated on the same avenue that led to the former Foreigner's Settlement, but west of St Nikita, is the splendidly baroque **Apraxin/Trubetskoi Mansion** (1769). It is unique in the city. Flush with the pavement, its blue walls offset by white detailing snake along the street where tired Muscovites huddle waiting for buses, oblivious to the grandeur behind them. The central section protrudes impishly and the corner porticoes are strongly defined with paired pilasters and broken pediments. Its joyous appearance and shape, enhanced by the unusual, bright colour, has led to its nickname *dom-commode* (chest-of-drawers). During its heyday as the Trubetskoi mansion, it was a centre of the literary salon of the early nineteenth century — Pushkin was a frequent visitor. In the 1860s no longer viable as a private house, it became the Fourth Boys' Gymnasium, where Stanislavsky studied, and which he found unbearably strict. After the Revolution the prestigious Industrial Academy was located here.

## MOSCOW REBORN

With the accession of Peter III in 1762, Moscow's slow revival quickened pace. This sickly, capricious young man, grandson of Peter the Great, was obsessed by admiration for Prussian military might. He became immensely unpopular when he recalled his army as it was on the verge of defeating Frederick the Great of Prussia, thereby depriving it of a great victory. His wife, Catherine, the daughter of a minor German prince, with the help of her lover, Gregory Orlov, and the Guards regiments he controlled, overthrew Peter only six months after he took the throne. Poor Peter, imprisoned on his estate at Ropsha, was eventually to die at the hands of his guards. During his short reign, however, he took some important decisions, including the abolition, except in time of war, of the rule whereby all members of the nobility were obliged to give service to the state. This released the upper class from their obligation to live near the court, and many took advantage of their new freedom to move to Moscow. Indeed, Catherine was to complain that her courtiers were always making excuses to leave the capital for the delights of the old city. Moscow provided a more open climate of opinion than St Petersburg, stifled by the proximity of the court. The first Russian university in the Empire had been founded in Moscow in 1755, during the reign of Elizabeth. (Part of it is still housed in the handsome classical building on the Mokhovaya facing the Kremlin.) Mikhail Lomonosov, the fisherman's son turned poet, scientist, philologist and genius of the age, became its first rector. The leading critical writers, Novikov, Fonvizin and Radishchev, all lived in or were focused on Moscow. With the return of the landed classes, new grand mansions appeared overlooking the Kremlin, on the fashionable road to the former Foreigner's Settlement and along the wide ring roads of earlier fortifications — Bely Gorod and the Garden Ring.

## FLIRTING WITH THE GOTHIC

Vasily Bazhenov, the greatest architect of this age, was a graduate of the Paris Academy and also studied in Rome. As court architect, he came to Moscow in 1769 under commission from Catherine to reconstruct the Kremlin. His plan was to surround the existing old buildings

with colonnades and new classical buildings, and he went so far as to demolish part of the south wall facing the river. The Empress even came to Moscow for the inauguration ceremony. But, happily for posterity, after three years Catherine lost interest in the project and Bazhenov had to make good the damage to the Kremlin — restore the section of demolished wall and fill in the foundations. There is a model of his bold but appalling conception of the colossal building in the Museum of Architecture.

**Tsaritsyno** Bazhenov then turned his genius to another palace for Catherine, in what was then countryside south of Moscow but is now within city limits. It was to be a grand estate for the Empress and her son, Paul, at Tsaritsyno in the newly fashionable 'Moorish-Gothic' style. Bazhenov worked on the project for ten years and when the red brick palace with white stone detailing was nearly complete, Catherine came to view it. Her displeasure, which reflected her poor relations with her son, meant Bazhenov was dismissed forthwith, the unsatisfactory palace was dismantled, and his rival, Matvei Kazakov, a former student of Prince Ukhtomsky, was appointed in his place. But Kazakov, too, was not allowed to finish the palace owing to the drain on the Treasury from the Turkish wars. The group of buildings, walls and bridges stood unfinished for more than two centuries, suffering from pilfering by local people and the ravages of time. It is a folly on a grand scale, but its roofless buildings and delightful bridge and gazebos, set above a wide, artificial lake, are still very beautiful. Since the Revolution various solutions have been

54. *The Tsar-bell, weighing over 200,000 kilograms, was cast in 1735 but broke in 1737, during a devastating fire, and has never been rung.*

55. *The Holy Well at the Danilov Monastery, rebuilt from ruins for the millennium of Christianity in Russia in 1988. The words say 'Look upon Thy People O Lord and Confirm Them in the True Faith'.*

suggested for the buildings — the Soviet leader Mikoyan thought they would make an ideal champagne factory — but nothing concrete resulted until in the Eighties Polish restorers set to work to renovate the buildings. A school of art is to open in the building originally intended as an opera house.

**Peter Travel Palace**  The talented Kazakov, best known as the designer of more than thirty great classical buildings in Moscow, also constructed another wonderful semi-Gothic palace in Moscow, north of the old city on the road to St Petersburg. The Peter Travel Palace (*Petrovsky Putevoi Zamok*) was intended to provide the Empress with a place to recover and change after the arduous journey on bad roads by carriage from St Petersburg. Round walls with towers like a medieval castle surround the red and white square palace with its great central

*56. Monument to the poet and diplomat Alexander Griboyedov (murdered in Persia in 1829) by A. Manuilov, erected in 1959.*

*57. Beyond the columns of the Trinity Church, built in 1833 by Osip Bove, can be seen the picturesque Cathedral of the Seven Ecumenical Councils (16th-18th century), which in the 1980s was wonderfully restored from ruins.*

rotunda under a hemispherical dome. It has borrowings from medieval Russian architecture, like the fat, melon-like columns of the porch and pendules. Inside the *trompe l'oeil* and sculptured decor is purely classical in style.

In 1812 Napoleon moved here with his suite when the flames of burning Moscow threatened to engulf the Kremlin. He watched the great fire from the palace; the sky glowed red for six long days. The palace was used by the tsars during coronations in Moscow, including that of Nicholas II and his wife, Alexandra, in 1896. Across the way were the Khodynka Fields, where gifts were to be distributed to a huge crowd after the ceremony. The horrified couple watched from the balcony as the crowd in their anxiety pushed and shoved until some fell into ditches and some two thousand people were trampled to death — a dreadful omen for the start of the reign.

# EARLY CLASSICAL MANSIONS

**Pashkov Mansion**   At the end of the eighteenth century, elegant grand mansions proliferated on the edges of the old centre. Moscow's most outstanding private house of this period is the Pashkov Mansion (1784-88). Its prominent situation, facing the Kremlin's western Borovitsky Gate and the Great Stone Bridge, lends it a majesty that is enhanced by the architecture. It was designed by Bazhenov, who remained in Moscow after his disagreements with the Empress to work for P. Pashkov, a wealthy nobleman, Captain of the Guard and descendant of Peter the Great's valet.

Its size, position and rich façade, with pediment, portico, sculpture and colonnade linking the wings to the central three-storey block, make it the leading house of this period. The entry to this fine house is from the courtyard behind, where there are high wrought-iron gates. The railings at the front were removed in 1930, when the street was widened and the clumsy stone steps were added.

The mansion remained in the hands of the Pashkovs for a relatively short time. Like many of the great houses built in Moscow at the end of the eighteenth century, it proved too large and expensive to maintain in the different conditions prevailing after the French invasion of 1812. Damaged in the great fire, it was carefully repaired and in 1839 was purchased as a school for sons of the nobility. In 1862 it became the famous Imperial Rumyantsev Museum, housing the collection of paintings and books belonging to the son of the famous General Rumyantsev.

After the Revolution, the mansion and the books formed the basis of the Lenin Library, now the Russian State Library. The interiors were significantly altered to suit its later functions and nothing survives of the original decor. Tragically, in 1985, when a fourth metro line was constructed under the building, serious damage was caused to its foundations. Repairs lasting many years were finally completed in 1994.

**Baryshnikov Mansion**   On Myasnitskaya, just north of the Boulevard, is a fine house set back from the street behind a generous driveway. It is the Baryshnikov Mansion (1797-1802), built by Matvei Kazakov in the form of a U, with the two wings connecting it with the street; the central part in the courtyard is composed of four Corinthian columns supporting a pediment. The fine reception rooms are to the left of the entrance and form a long *enfilade*, starting with the formal bedroom with elegant painted and plastered ceilings and leading to the oval-shaped ballroom with slender Corinthian columns.

The house, which remained in the Baryshnikov family until the 1840s, was often visited by the great satirist and poet Griboyedov, a friend of the Baryshnikovs' son-in-law. He was working at that time on his masterpiece, *Woe from Wit*, which, in brilliant rhyming couplets, describes Moscow society of the 1820s. Griboyedov suffered a horrible death when, as Russian envoy to Persia just after his marriage to a beautiful Georgian princess, he was torn limb from limb by an enraged crowd.

**Catherine Palace**   Currently in use by the Russian military as an academy is the monumental Catherine Palace in Lefortovo, across the Yauza River in east Moscow, not far from the former Foreigners' Settlement. The two outstanding Italian architects of Catherine's court,

*58. The Russian defeat of Napoleon's army in 1812 was celebrated by the construction of the Triumphal Arch (1834), designed by Osip Bove with sculptures by Vitali and Timofeyev. Built of stone with cast-iron columns and figures, it was dismantled in 1936 but re-erected in 1968.*

*59. Detail of the Triumphal Arch.*

60. The Chariot of Glory, its six
mounts straining at the reins,
stands at the top of the
Triumphal Arch.

*61, 62. At the base of General Kutuzov's statue, sculpted by Nikolai Tomsky in 1973, the Russian soldiers on the left have their rifles at the ready while French officers with Napoleon, centre, look on disdainfully.*

63-70. Moscow's buildings, especially those within the old city, display great variety of colour and style, from the serenely classical to the exuberant neo-baroque, through curvaceous Art Nouveau to the sombre pilasters and heavy capitals of the Soviet monumental style.

71. The Bolshoi, Moscow's oldest and leading opera and ballet theatre, was founded in the 18th century by an English entrepreneur. The present building constructed in 1856 by Albert Cavos was modelled on an earlier theatre of 1824 which had been destroyed by fire.

Antonio Rinaldi and Giacomo Quarenghi, played a major role in its construction, which took over twenty years (1773-96). Its splendid interiors were lost in 1797, when Paul I turned it into a barracks, which later housed the crack Cadet Corps. After the Revolution it became a tank corps academy bearing Stalin's name. The incredibly long colonnade and loggia of 16 Corinthian columns and the end porticoes are Quarenghi's work.

**Museum of the Revolution** The mansion used by Tolstoy as the model for the house of Pierre Bezukhov in *War and Peace* is in central Moscow on the main street, Tverskaya. With its long red façade set back behind railings and strange, grinning lions at the gates, it immediately attracts attention. Built in 1780 for the Kheraskov family, it was badly damaged in the 1812 fire. Restored afterwards by the British architect Adam Menelaws, in 1831 it became the exclusive English Club — based on the London clubs — for members of the Russian nobility. Some of the interiors survive from this time. In the 1920s it became the Museum of the Revolution. Struggling to survive in the post-Soviet era, the museum now includes exhibitions about the attempted coup of August 1991 among its displays.

There are many other classical mansions in Moscow. They include the former Alexandra Palace, used by the tsars as a Moscow residence, now inhabited by the Academy of Sciences, with fine interiors and even some of the original furniture and paintings. The vastly wealthy Demidov family owned several such mansions; one, in eastern Moscow, is notable for its severe façade and contrasting richly gilded and decorated interior. It is remarkable that the institutions which use these buildings have not substantially damaged the interiors.

*72. Tchaikovsky's Swan Lake, first performed at the Bolshoi in 1877, is still a mainstay of its repertory.*

*73. Fyodor Chaliapin, the magnificent bass, was from 1899 to 1917 soloist at the Bolshoi, where he was famous for his roles as Boris Godunov and Mephistopheles.*

## COUNTRY ESTATES

A few large eighteenth-century estates are now entirely surrounded by new Moscow. They make wonderful public parks, places of refuge in the desert of ugly, poor-quality tower blocks that surround them on all sides.

**Razumovsky Estate**  The Razumovsky Mansion lies on the banks of the Yauza River just outside the Garden Ring in eastern Moscow. It was built in 1803 by the British architect Adam Menelaws, not of stone but, surprisingly, of wood covered with an outside layer of stucco. Amazingly, in this city of frequent fires, it has survived (the fire of 1812 did not reach this part of Moscow). The elaborate portico with Ionic columns forms the grand centre of the house and the wings, originally separate, are now connected and extend in a wide U to the street. Count Alexei Kirillovich Razumovsky, the owner, was a son of Kirill Razumovsky, the choir boy from the Ukraine who so took Empress Elizabeth's fancy that she married him morganatically in a church in Moscow. Alexei's brother, Count Andrei Kirillovich, appointed Russian Ambassador to Vienna by Catherine, was a keen musician and friend of Beethoven, who dedicated the Razumovsky Quartets to him. The great house, which had an extensive park down to the Yauza River, proved too large for one family and was purchased by the state for an orphanage in the second half of the nineteenth century. In Soviet times it has served as the Institute of Physical Education, although it now stands empty, waiting for new owners.

**Kuskovo**  Another such estate, Kuskovo, almost at the eastern border of the present city, belonged to Count Pyotr Sheremetiev, son of Field

Marshal Boris Sheremetiev, who headed the army under Peter the Great. Kuskovo, built over forty years (1740-80) by a group of French and Russian architects, among whom were Sheremetiev serfs, is the grandest of the estates of the nobility, the 'Versailles' of the Moscow countryside. It remained in the Sheremetiev family until 1918. The huge and wonderful public park of the present day is composed of woods, a large lake overlooked by the main house and church, a Dutch house, grotto, Italian cottage, green theatre, hermitage, orangerie, and even special houses for animals and birds. The gardens are full of statuary. The rooms in the single-storey main house are richly decorated, the original furniture is still *in situ*, and the curtains and wall hangings, skilfully renewed over the years, are all in place.

The house, neither large nor monumental, has a modest portico with pediment approached by a driveway on either side. It is harmonious, 'human' in its scale, a welcoming place that does not overwhelm. Built of wood and used only as a summer retreat, it nevertheless has magnificent stoves in the principal rooms. In the grounds the most impressive pavilion is the grotto, designed by the serf-architect Fyodor Arguno (1771), with wonderful shell work by Johannes Fokt.

To the chagrin of his family, Nikolai, Count Pyotr Sheremetiev's son, fell in love with Praskovia Zhemchugova-Kovalyeva, an actress in his father's theatre. The young Count built for her at Ostankino another magnificent house, which served equally as a retreat and a splendid theatre.

**Ostankino**  The palace at Ostankino is now surrounded by blocks of flats, noisy trams rattle past its front garden, and the television tower rises high over the lake. Its Church of the Trinity was built in 1688, when the estate belonged to the Cherkassky princes. The church's elaborate patterned brickwork and fine carved stone detailing, its peaked porch, rows of gables and bulbous cupolas make a strong foil to the classical features of the later palace. It is just this combination of styles from different centuries that gives Moscow its vividness.

The Italians Camporezi, Quarenghi and Brenna contributed to the design of the wooden palace (1792-98), but the same serf-architects who worked at Kuskovo supervised the construction. Like Kuskovo intended only for use in the summer, it is made up of a series of elaborate state rooms which lead one into the other until the central hall, replete with paintings from the Count's splendid collection, is reached. The two-storey great hall under a shallow dome is entered through double doors. It has the capacity to be transformed into a theatre or back into a ballroom in half an hour; the machinery to make all this happen still exists within the walls. In the wings are the splendidly decorated Egyptian concert hall and the Italian pavilion crammed with antique sculpture.

The strong feeling of stepping back into history is enhanced not only by the sight of the furniture, hangings and paintings, silent witnesses to the life of two hundred years ago, but now also by the occasional charming concerts of eighteenth-century music and opera given in the heat of the Moscow summer.

The theatrical troupe existed until 1801, when Praskovia and the Count married secretly in Moscow. But she enjoyed only two years of married life; in 1803, just after the birth of their son, Dmitry, she died. A

few years later the Count also died, and the baby was left a rich orphan. In later life, at meetings in this palace Count Dmitry Sheremetiev, son of a former serf, advised Alexander II on the problems of the emancipation, which Alexander declared in 1861. Immediately after the Revolution, the palace was made into a museum and its contents preserved.

# PUBLIC HOSPITALS

In the last quarter of the eighteenth century wealthy patrons began to provide much needed hospitals and almshouses to supplement those included within poorhouse establishments organised by the Church. Many of these charitable institutions are still functioning as hospitals today.

**Sheremetiev Hospital**  Count Nikolai Sheremetiev's grief at the loss of his actress-wife was somewhat assuaged by the building of the great charity hospital on the northern side of the Garden Ring, begun in 1794 to the design of Yelezvoi Nazarov. When his wife died in 1803, Sheremetiev dedicated the entire hospital to her and invited the great Quarenghi to design the portico. Quarenghi is responsible for the wonderful semi-circular double colonnade of the portico that ushers one into the church in the exact centre of the building under the shallow cupola. Ivan Scotti executed the fine frescoes. Now the Sklifosovsky Institute, the hospital has modern additions at the back, and uses the old entrance with the chapel as a museum of medicine.

**Golitsyn Hospital**  One of the best works of Matvei Kazakov is the Golitsyn Hospital (1801), built in the form of a palatial estate with an

austere façade and wings extending forward on either side to embrace the courtyard. The central section under the broad shallow cupola at the top of a flight of steps is the rotunda church, defined by an interior colonnade of slender Ionic columns. The free hospital and almshouse were the gift of Prince Dmitry Golitsyn, Russian Ambassador in Vienna before Razumovsky. His tomb originally lay in the chapel but was removed to the Archangel Church in the Don Monastery, along with numerous other Golitsyn tombs, when the church was closed after the Revolution. In 1991 services recommenced in the chapel.

## CHURCHES

**St Philip**  Classical churches of the late eighteenth century, like mansions and public buildings, were almost the preserve of the energetic and talented Kazakov. The rotunda church of St Philip the Metropolitan

*75. The 18th-century formal gardens at the Sheremetiev estate at Kuskovo were so clearly inspired by French models that they were known as the Russian Versailles.*

*76. Sculpture, an important feature of the Kuskovo gardens, became very popular in Russia during the 1800s.*

(*Filippa Mitropolita*, 1777-88) is one of his earlier works. It was the local church for the parishioners of a wealthy district of Moscow, the Pervaya Meshchanskaya (Prospekt Mira). The then unusual rotunda, joined to the slightly older refectory and bell tower, is awash with marvellous bas-reliefs and porticoes of Doric columns, giving a decidedly secular air. The rather confined circular interior with its coffered ceiling and sculptured cornice is defined by columns of the Ionic order reminiscent of the great hall of the Senate building in the Kremlin, also by Kazakov. In 1991, the church reopened for services.

**Large Church of the Ascension** At Nikitsky Gate, facing the Boulevard, is a splendid white church, the Large Church of the Ascension (*Bolshovo Vozneseniya*) — the smaller and older Ascension Church is a few yards away on Herzen Street. A long time in the building, it was begun in 1798, interrupted by the French invasion in 1812, and not finally completed until 1840. Its form is simple: a cube support-

ing a broad green dome, with a single round apse jutting out from the east side, and on the west the entrance or *trapeznaya*. Porticoes define the north and south entrances. It is an excellent example of the mature classical style in Moscow, carefully balanced both vertically with the broad dome and horizontally where the refectory complements the apse.

Prince Grigory Potemkin, one of Catherine's principal favourites, commissioned the grand church designed by the St Petersburg architect, Ivan Starov, in 1798. The 1812 fire so damaged the incomplete structure that it was not until 1829 that its construction was again tackled by a new architect, F. Shestakov, although since 1816 two side chapels had been in use. It was in one of these that Russia's greatest poet, Alexander Pushkin, married Natalia Goncharova in 1831. Finally, the city architect in charge of the restoration of Moscow, Osip Bove, added the two porticoes on the north and south, and it was at last finally ready in 1840.

It was to function for less than a century; in the 1930s it was closed, its bell tower demolished, and it was handed over to the Moscow electricity services. In the Eighties a campaign was launched to turn the church into a concert hall. It was only when Boris Yeltsin, First Party Secretary for Moscow in 1985, stormed into the church personally and gave the electricity authorities a week to clear out that they finally left. The church is now holding services again, although the elaborate interior was completely ruined.

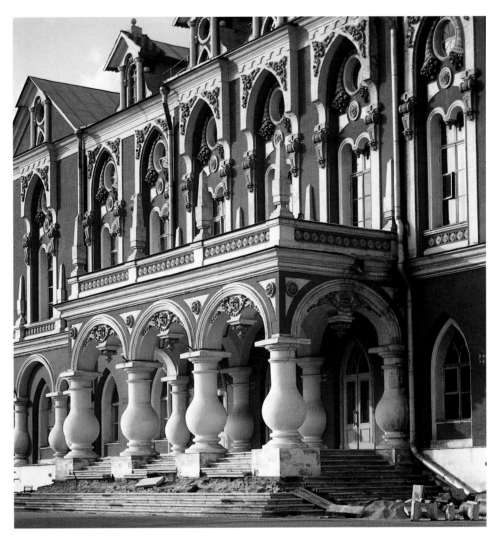

*78. The Peter Palace was built (1776-82) in the reign of Catherine II by Matvei Kazakov. He was Moscow's foremost classical architect, but here he employed a successful mixture of Russian medieval forms in the bulbous columns and hanging penduls, and the Gothic style in the arched windows and towers.*

## NAPOLEON, THE FIRE, AND ITS AFTERMATH

At the head of his vast army, Napoleon invaded Russia in June 1812. By September he reached Borodino, on the doorstep of Moscow, where an inconclusive battle was fought, though the Russian troops retreated, leaving the way clear for the Emperor to enter the city. But nearly everyone had left Moscow. Before the first night was out, a conflagration began, most likely started by Russian incendiaries. The fire burned for six days, consuming two-thirds of the city. For Napoleon it spelled disaster; all the winter supplies had been destroyed and he could no longer stay in the ruined town. After only thirty-three days he and his *Grande Armée* withdrew, so harassed by Russian troops that only one-tenth of those who crossed the border in June survived to recross it in October.

The city that emerged from these devastating times was greatly changed. Reconstruction was energetically tackled and achieved over a ten- to fifteen-year period. The new and restored houses were built of brick or stone, but also of wood, the favourite and cheapest material. Stucco houses of this period, although they look like stone or brick, were usually built of timber with daub and wattle under the plaster. The new houses were smaller, more compact and with attractive detailing — mouldings and window frames — that were missing from the grander, more strictly classical mansions of the previous generation. This style became known as Russian Empire. Tsar Alexander I took a great interest in the renewal of the city, even making suggestions as to the colours of the new houses; he preferred soft pastels to harsh reds and greens.

The city fathers, under the expert eye of Osip Bove, the chief architect of the renewed city, took advantage of the situation to partially redesign the centre, though keeping the circular-radial pattern. The moat in Red Square was filled in, the boulevards along the line of the old walls of Bely Gorod were completed, and the polluted Neglinnaya River that ran along the west side of the Kremlin was put in conduits underground allowing space for broad new squares, including the handsome Theatre Square.

**Lopukhin House**  The rebuilt city in the softer version of classicism was more charming, more on a human scale, than the pre-fire Moscow. Of the many attractive new houses, the Lopukhin House on Prechistenka, west of the Kremlin, is a splendid example. (The Lopukhins were descendants of Peter the Great's first wife.) Designed by Afanasy Grigoriev (1817-22), it is both modest and elegant. Having only one floor on the street side (and two floors for ordinary living on the courtyard), it has eleven windows that look out from the lofty reception rooms. The central five are framed by a portico of six Ionic columns supporting a broad pediment. The fine plaster mouldings behind the columns are the *leitmotif* of the Empire period.

**Khrushchev House**  A short block away is another outstanding example of Russian Empire style. The Khrushchev House (no connection with Nikita Khrushchev!), also by Grigoriev, was built in 1817 on a corner property with two equally impressive façades, an open porch on the side street with four pairs of Ionic columns and lovely sculptured bas reliefs and, facing the main road, six Ionic columns supporting a balcony with pediment. A large garden originally stood behind the house, taking up the entire block. In 1896 the house became an orphanage for children of the nobility and in the 1920s a famous toy museum was opened there. It is now the Pushkin Museum, devoted to the life of the poet, although he never visited the house.

**Church of the Consolation of All Sorrows**  Perhaps the most beautiful of the classical churches in Moscow is the Church of the Consolation of All Sorrows (*Vsekh Skorbyashchikh Radosti*) in the Zamoskvoreche area south of the Kremlin. It is a fine example of two of the best classical architects unwittingly co-operating to present a wonderfully harmonious whole. Vasily Bazhenov built the round bell tower and entrance (1783-91) for Dolgov, a merchant and his father-in-law, who lived across the street.

Fifty years later, Osip Bove, the city architect and restorer of Moscow, replaced the medieval church on this site with a new church much more appropriate for Bazhenov's bell tower. It has a tall dome supported by a broad drum pierced with windows over a rotunda, tall arched windows enlivened by columns, and the fine plasterwork characteristic of the Empire period. Within, the round central part of the church under the dome is defined by an elegant circle of Ionic columns that support a frieze. Even the circular iron floor is of the period. Though it was closed from 1937 to 1948, its iconostasis and interior decor did not suffer. Its priest, elected to the local council when free elections were held in 1990,

*79. The Apraksin/Trubetskoi mansion (1769), one of Moscow's few examples of western baroque, with its paired pilasters, sculptured window designs, and undulating façade.*

is a popular figure.

**The Bolshoi** The most successful of the new squares built after the French invasion is the great Theatre Square, its spaciousness derived from land reclaimed from the Neglinnaya River when it was placed in underground conduits. In 1824 the massive form of the Bolshoi (Large) Theatre was erected at the head of the rectangular square on the site of the former Petrovsky Theatre, a large wooden theatre cum dance hall which had burnt to the ground in 1805, leaving its English entrepreneur, Michael Maddox, utterly bankrupt. The new theatre, strictly classical in form, with its eight columns and Apollo riding his chariot above, was designed by Andrei Mikhailov from St Petersburg, together with Bove.

In 1853 the building caught fire while orphans from the Foundling Home were on stage; happily, the orphans were saved, but the theatre was left with only the walls standing. In a relatively short time it was rebuilt in a somewhat drier manner by Albert Cavos, the authority on acoustics and architect of the similar Mariinsky Theatre in St Petersburg. The spacious interior, which holds nearly three thousand people, is resplendent in the rich baroque style of red velvet, heavily ornamented plasterwork and gilt carving. The royal box at the back has seen many distinguished occupants: Tsars Alexander II and III, and Nicholas II, Lenin, Stalin, most of the members of the Politburo, Khrushchev, Brezhnev, Gorbachev, and their many guests, including latterly Ronald Reagan and Margaret Thatcher. The late nineteenth century, when Tchaikovsky, Rimsky-Korsakov and Mussorgsky were writing operas and ballets, was the golden age of the Bolshoi. After the Revolution it was at first a venue for political meetings, but was eventually reopened as a theatre. In this century it has staged many important premieres of major works by, among others, Prokofiev and Shostakovich.

# WOODEN EMPIRE

Wooden houses of the post-fire period are especially enchanting. In Maly Vlasevsky Lane (Taneevykh) there is a small frame house with a mezzanine: five windows on the ground floor with three above and entry from the courtyard. It is enhanced by a broad stone frieze on the façade and stone window lion masks. It was built in 1820 for a certain P. Fyodorov to a mass-produced plan of the Commission for the Construction of the City of Moscow.

Another delightful wooden dwelling is the Sytin House in Sytin Lane, just behind the new McDonald's on Pushkin Square. It, too, has one floor and a mezzanine, and a splendid frieze, although at the back, where wings extend into the courtyard, it is divided into three floors. It was built in 1811 and somehow escaped destruction in the fire of a year later.

The most unusual of the wooden houses of this period is surely the Orlov Dacha, often called 'dovecote' because of its appearance. Built by the Orlov counts as their summer house, it is set on a square stone ground floor, over which wooden columns circle the rotunda of the main first floor, topped by another tier and small dome. Its charm is nowadays somewhat obscured by factories and the peeling flats of the Sixties.

# VICTORY

To mark the great victory over the French in 1812, a triumphal arch was designed by Osip Bove to stand at the top of Tverskaya Street, near where the Belorussian Station is today. The great arch of stone with figures and decor of iron has at the top an angel representing Glory riding a chariot and below, groups of soldiers illustrating the defeat of the French. It stood at the Belorussian Station until 1936, when it was taken down and packed into boxes, not destroyed as were so many monuments at that time. In 1968 it was re-erected, but not on its original site, at the commencement of Kutuzovsky Prospekt in the south-west, on the route Napoleon chose to enter Moscow.

Nicholas I decided to build a more impressive monument to the victory over Napoleon. After several false starts, a mammoth church, the **Cathedral of Christ the Redeemer** (*Khrista Spasitelya*), designed by Konstantin Ton in pseudo-Russian style, was erected on the banks of the Moskva River just west of the Kremlin. It took fifty years to build and was so large that it dominated everything in the vicinity, including the Kremlin. It functioned for just another fifty years, until blown up in 1931 to provide a site for the projected monumental Palace of Soviets. But this, too, was doomed to failure.

# MERCANTILE MOSCOW

The conservative Tsar Nicholas I, who died in 1856, was succeeded by his son, Alexander II. In spite of his conventional militarily oriented upbringing, Alexander differed greatly from his autocratic father. He began his reign in a positive manner by agreeing to terms that ended the

*81. Columns and alcoves were very fashionable in Moscow interiors of the early 19th century, especially in the reconstruction of the city after the great fire in 1812.*

*82. Columns proliferate, too, in church architecture as here, where Ionic columns contrast with Corinthian and the curves of the corner. This part of the Church of the Consolation of All Sorrows was the work of the talented architect Vasily Bazhenov, in 1791.*

disastrous Crimean War. Although he remained an autocrat to the end, and was finally assassinated by young revolutionaries after several bungled attempts, significant reforms were introduced during his reign and he justly deserved the title 'Tsar-Liberator'.

Under the feudal system that prevailed in Russia until 1861, most of the population were landless peasants tied to their lord and obliged to work his lands. In that year Alexander II, opposing the wishes of the landed gentry, finally enacted the order for the emancipation of the peasants. Although the legal and administrative reforms of Alexander's reign were also important, the act of emancipation was fundamental in propelling Russia towards rapid industrial development. The second most important factor in boosting the economy was the building of the railways. The construction of the Siberian line at the end of the century effectively gave the Russian economy access to huge Asian markets, which stimulated stupendous growth in manufacture, particularly of the textile industry. Finally, the rise of a group of remarkable entrepreneurs from the hardworking peasantry, many of Old Believer stock, provided the imagination and drive to exploit the new economic conditions. It is not always realised that Russia's exceptional growth was such that in 1914 it was the fourth largest industrial power in the world.

Moscow, the centre of productivity and trade, reflected these boom conditions in growth of population and expansion. Its population of 400,000 in 1862 had leaped to over a million by the end of the century. If in the past, the control of government and the economy had been in the hands of the land-owning nobility, in the second half of the nineteenth century the initiative passed firmly to the new merchant class. Often former serfs, many of the new merchants had had the energy and initiative

to purchase their freedom before emancipation and set up small businesses in the cities. With the release of labour from the countryside after
1861, their businesses grew apace and some, having begun life in
bondage, died millionaires.

This new breed with plenty of money to spend wanted a new kind
of architecture to express their individuality. The classical period, now in
its dying throes, was too closely associated with the old nobility. So the
*nouveau-riche* enthusiastically adopted the flowing curves of Art
Nouveau or the quaintness of the pseudo-Russian style when planning
their grand houses in Moscow. At the end of the century the municipali-
ty, by then elected on a limited franchise, began constructing elaborate
public buildings, mostly in pseudo-Russian style, that transformed the
centre of Moscow.

## PUBLIC BUILDINGS

One of the reforms introduced by Alexander II was the election of
town councils chosen on a property franchise and headed by elected
mayors (*golova*). The Moscow town council or *duma*, in which the new
business class, the 'merchants', predominated, decided to construct a
splendid new building, the Duma, at the entrance to Red Square for their
meetings and offices. They took as their *leitmotif* sixteenth- and seventeenth-century Russian architecture. Built in 1890-92 by Dmitry
Chichagov, it is a block with large arched central windows and an
entrance porch replete with ogee gables, pendules and the melon-like
columns of old Russia. The red brick façade is busy with other medieval
motifs. It is rather strident and cumbersome, but the porch and the

85. Count Nikolai Sheremetiev
built the sumptuous wooden
palace cum theatre at Ostankino
in 1798 for his bride, the serf-
actress and singer, Praskovia. It
was designed by leading architects of Italian origin,
Camporezzi, Quarenghi and
Brenna, and a number of
Sheremetiev serf-architects. It is
one of Moscow's most splendid
museums, in which the furniture,
paintings and sculpture are still
intact.

86. More ordinary people lived
in wooden houses like this one
on Maly Vlasevsky Lane built
(1820) for P. Fyodorov. The
mezzanine, the lion masks and
the frieze are typical of small
houses of this period.

strongly peaked roofs with iron railings are attractive.

From 1936 to 1993 it was used as the Lenin Museum, its 36 halls displaying objects and reconstructions from Lenin's life. Among the more interesting exhibits was his Rolls Royce, a Silver Cloud Alpine Eagle. In the early 90s a vociferous group of supporters of the old Soviet regime liked to gather daily on the porch to discuss their grievances in the light of the demise of the Soviet Union. In November 1993 the museum was closed and the building given over to the History Museum.

**Red Square** New public buildings in the 1880s transformed the north and east side of Red Square. The **History Museum** (1878-83) illustrates the growing preoccupation with Russian history at that time. Through the vehicle of the Archaeological Society, new discoveries had been made and collections amassed which led to the idea of a central museum. Vladimir Sherwood (Shervud in Russian — his antecedents came to Russia in the eighteenth century) won the competition for the façade together with the engineer A. Semyonov. Although inside it has well-lit halls decorated in an interesting neo-Russian manner, its façade, a hodgepodge of ancient Russian motifs in unattractive red brick (Sherwood would have preferred coloured tiles) looks decidedly lugubrious in comparison with the magnificence of St Basil's at the other end of the square. Still, it is a stunning museum, which regrettably has been closed for the past seven years for repairs.

Red Square was enhanced by another, unique building. The Upper Trading Rows, or **GUM** (State Universal Store) as it is commonly known today, is merely the last in a series of market buildings and arcades that have stood on this site since the earliest times. After the 1812 fire, Osip Bove built a stone arcade, which in 1888 was replaced by Alexander Pomerantsev's spectacular building. In answer to the need to provide a multitude of shops, he designed three passageways roofed over by a revolutionary broad span of glass. Thus, there are over a thousand different stalls in this two-storey structure, lit brilliantly from above, with wide aisles and an elegant fountain in the centre. It is Moscow's most successful shop. But its complex façade of grey, poorly delineated stone, fails as a foil to the Kremlin opposite.

Reopened after the Revolution as GUM, it was closed in 1930 and used by government organisations involved in central economic planning. In 1932, after her suicide, the body of Stalin's wife, Nadezhda Alliluyeva, was brought here to lie in state. Stalin stood brooding by her body, narrowly watching which Party leaders came to pay their respects; those who failed to do so were marked men during the purges a few years later. In 1953, after Stalin died, GUM reopened.

**Sandunov Baths** Not far from Red Square, on Neglinnaya Street, is a strange arched 'Moorish' entrance leading into a courtyard more in keeping with Central Asia than Moscow. Of all Moscow's sixty steam baths, the Sandunov (*Sandunovskye Bani*) are the most magnificent. The Moorish courtyard was built on the street side for shops and apartments, while the baths with their richly decorated halls lie behind, across a little lane, the steam in winter seeming to hang in the cold air. It is a Russian tradition not dulled by modern bathrooms to use steam baths at least once a week, preferably on Saturday, as the only way to properly clean the pores. The suffocating steam room has steps to allow one to rise

87. The History Museum (1833) guards one end of Red Square and St Basil's the other. Designed by Vladimir Sherwood, of English origin, it imitates the motifs of the Kremlin and St Basil's in a heavy, theatrical way.

higher and higher into the cloud of hot steam. After that comes a dip in the cold pool, and a repeat of the torture. Russians look upon the baths as a sort of social club; the warm relaxed feeling afterwards is conducive to deep conversation, especially if a little vodka is on hand.

**Neo-Baroque Mansions**  On the Prechistenka, west of the Kremlin, sprinkled in among elegant Empire mansions are more richly attired neo-baroque houses of the late nineteenth century. No. 20, a jewel-like house squeezed between two larger mansions, is typically encrusted with baroque flourishes. It was given to the dancer Isadora Duncan, an admirer of the Bolsheviks, when she spontaneously decided to throw in her lot with them and set up a dancing school in Moscow. Originally built at the beginning of the nineteenth century, the house was transformed in 1910 by the wealthy merchant, A.K. Ushkov, for his ballerina wife, Alexandra Balashova, the star of the Bolshoi. With its ornate iron balconies and mass of sculptural detail, it immediately attracts attention on this unparalleled street of fine houses. In 1921 Isadora established her school for needy children who lived as well as danced there. It was here that she met and impulsively married the handsome poet, Sergei Yesenin, although they never spoke each other's language. The stormy marriage ended in 1924; a year later the talented Yesenin shot himself in the Hotel Angleterre in Leningrad.

Another of these heavily sculpted houses that abound in the old districts of Moscow is the ornate mansion with tower and paired columns built in 1897 by Sergei Sherwood, son of the designer of the History Museum, for M. Rekk, a wealthy entrepreneur who profited from the property boom of those years. After the Revolution it was used as the headquarters of the Zamoskvoreche section of the Communist Party and was once visited by Lenin.

**House of Friendship/Morozov**  On the Vozdvizhenka near the Kremlin is a strange-looking mansion, resembling a castle more than a town house. It has a doorway of twin towers crowned by lacy stonework, sea shells climb the walls, and a twisted rope motif forms the columns. It was built for the playboy Arseny, fourth generation of the Abram branch of the Morozovs, whose fortune lay in the textile industry. His mother, Barbara, a formidable blue-stocking, lived next door and built this strange house for her errant son in 1898. It was designed by the mystic architect, V. Mazyrin, and based on the Palacio de Pena at Sintra in Portugal, seen by both Arseny and Mazyrin on their travels. Arseny, given to boasting, shot himself in the foot to demonstrate his strong nerves. As a result, he died of blood poisoning aged only twenty-nine in 1903. The house and part of his considerable fortune remained in the hands of his mistress, Mme Konshina; his wife and daughter inherited the rest.

After the Revolution, in 1918, anarchists seized the mansion and held it for a few months during their brief ascendancy. It then became the new Proletkult, an organisation set up to develop a specifically workers' culture. In this capacity the strange house witnessed many interesting events. Lunacharsky, the Minister for Enlightenment, disputed with the poet of the Revolution, Mayakovsky; Eisenstein and Meyerhold staged their avant-garde plays; and poets of the stature of Yesenin read their work. It was for a time the cultural centre of the new regime. After the war it became the House of Friendship, headquarters of the front organisation promoting good relations with other countries. Its interiors have

survived virtually intact; there are breathtaking reception rooms decorated in various styles with painted ceilings and marvellous plasterwork.

## NEO-RUSSIAN

The closer interest in Russian history in the latter part of the nineteenth century led to the use of themes of sixteenth- and seventeenth-century architecture. The *izba* or wooden house decorated in peasant style designed in the 1850s for Mikhail Pogodoin, the historian and Slavophile, is an example of the revival of interest in things Russian. The crude application of these forms is known as the pseudo-Russian style — exemplified by the façade of the History Museum, GUM, and the Lenin Museum. Perhaps the most fantastic example is the amazing **Igumnov House** on the Yakimanka, which looks like an apparition out of a fairy tale. Designed by the Yaroslavl architect Nikolai Pozdeyev and completed in 1893, it makes use of every conceivable theme: pendules, indented brick niches, ogee shapes, towers, bulbous roofs, window designs, tiles and ornamental brick. The main hall is an outstandingly good representation of a medieval hall, with painted flower and plant designs in many vivid colours and small and large doorways. Other rooms, heavy with plaster work, are more contemporary in style. The Igumnovs hardly used this large house and in the 1930s it became the French Embassy; latterly, it is the residence of the French ambassador. The talented pre- and post-Revolution architect Alexei Shchusev, as a young man about to choose a career as an artist, was so impressed by this house that he chose architecture instead.

**Tretyakov Art Gallery** The neo-Russian style differs from the

pseudo-Russian in that medieval architectural forms were more freely employed in a new, but historically familiar manner. The artist Viktor Vasnetsov's design for the façade of the Tretyakov Gallery (1905) is an outstanding example of this trend. Pavel Tretyakov, member of a merchant family, became a passionate collector of Russian art and gathered together a notable collection of paintings of the eighteenth and nineteenth centuries in his own home. After his death, the collection was given to the city of Moscow and Vasnetsov's new façade and extra galleries were added. The house has been adapted so many times to accommodate the paintings that it is unrecognisable as a nineteenth-century mansion. The brilliant red and white entrance is divided by a frieze and central ogee-shaped gable depicting St George and the Dragon, the symbol of the city. Peaked window frames and the triple entry porch are familiar themes done in a lively manner. The inscription above the frieze describes the gallery as the gift of Pavel and Sergei (his brother) Tretyakov.

The gallery, under restoration for nine long years, is now open again. It contains the best icon collection in the world (many, of course, confiscated from churches). Icons such as the Old Testament Trinity by Rublev and the original Virgin of Vladimir are especially revered. Other paintings include important portraits by Repin, Serov and Kramskoy, the huge religious paintings of Ivanov, *genre* paintings by Malyavin, Vasnetsov and Polenov, landscapes by Shishkin and Levitan, and works by the anti-war artist Vereshchagin. There are also paintings by the important Art Nouveau artist Mikhail Vrubel, the dream-like symbolist pictures of Borisov-Musatov, the symbolist-religious art of Petrov-Vodkin, and the avant-garde art of Chagall.

**Pertsov Apartment House** In the early years of the twentieth century, artists of a new and exciting generation flocked to Moscow and joined various modern groups in their urge to turn away from the strictly academic, classical style that had for so long dominated the Russian art world. There were many artists in this new wave who later became world famous: Kasimir Malevich, Alexander Rodchenko, his wife Varvara Stepanova, Lyubov Popova, Natalia Goncharova, Mikhail Larionov, Vladimir Tatlin, to name but a few. Their avant-garde art was not universally well received, but they held exhibitions, now regarded as milestones, and linked up with similar movements in the literary scene. Some of them lived in an amazing apartment block especially designed for artists. This is the Pertsov House, situated on the Moskva River not far from the west tower of the Kremlin. It has wonderful views. The ceramic panels that fill the gables of the steeply pitched roof and the dragons and other fantastic details were designed by the Arts and Crafts movement artist, Sergei Malyutin, to illustrate Russian fairy tales. A colourful and unusual design has been grafted onto what otherwise would have been an ordinary apartment block. Within, one apartment was decorated in similar folklore fashion.

**Martha-Mary Community** New churches, too, were exhibiting the influence of medieval architecture in exciting ways. One of the most beautiful is the **Cathedral of the Intercession** (*Pokrova*) from 1911, designed by Alexei Shchusev for the Martha-Mary Community, a religious sisterhood. The Grand Duchess Elizabeth, sister of the Empress and therefore both aunt and sister-in-law of Nicholas II, founded the convent after the tragic death of her husband. Moscow in 1905 exploded with industrial and political unrest. Simmering discontent was triggered into violence by the failures of the Russian forces in the 1904-05 war with Japan, especially after the sinking of the Russian fleet at Port Arthur. This first revolution started in January after news came to Moscow about 'Bloody Sunday', the massacre of peaceful demonstrators on 9 January in St Petersburg. On 4 February 1905 the Governor General of Moscow, Grand Duke Sergei Alexandrovich, uncle of the Emperor, was murdered by a bomb laid just inside the Nikolsky Gate of the Kremlin. In the autumn the conflict came to a head; there was shooting in the streets, barricades were built, but the superior force of troops brought from the capital finally and with great cruelty overcame the revolt. Grand Duchess Elizabeth retired to the convent.

The church is quite simply wonderful. The central cube, porch, twin entrance towers, and stone inscriptions, are borrowed from Russian medieval architecture. Its most dominant feature is the unusually large drum and corpulent, pointed cupola that is not quite onion-shaped. Its inspiration would seem to stem from the early squat bulbous churches of Pskov, but the proportions are greatly exaggerated. For a time after the Revolution the church was used as a cinema, but since 1945 the state restoration studio has been in occupation, its large ancient icons stacked about the nave contrasting strongly with the Art Nouveau paintings by Nesterov on the walls. The studio is moving to other premises and the church is again holding services.

The Grand Duchess lived in one of the surrounding buildings, devoting herself with the nuns to looking after the poor and needy, orphans, down-and-outs and, after 1914, wounded soldiers from the front. In 1918 with other members of the royal family she was taken to a place near Yekaterinburg and most cruelly murdered by being thrown down a well into which acid was poured.

**Railways** In the railway boom of the second half of the nineteenth century, nine impressive railway stations were constructed in a circle around Moscow, linked by a now under-used circular railway. The stations in pseudo- and neo-Russian, pseudo-Byzantine or neo-classical styles, were all imposing edifices. At Kalanchevskaya (Komsomolskaya) Square in north-eastern Moscow are grouped three contrasting stations: the old classical Nikolai Station (1851) by Konstantin Ton, for trains to St Petersburg; the Yaroslavl by Fyodor Shekhtel in striking neo-Russian style, for trains to the north; and the attractive Kazan, by Shchusev (1913-26), for trains to Central Asia. The Kazan's sentimental entrance wall, originally red and white, is imitative of seventeenth-century Moscow baroque and earlier Russian styles. The four-tiered entrance tower with spire is borrowed from the Kazan Kremlin.

The Yaroslavl Station, built in 1904 by Fyodor Shekhtel, takes the neo-Russian style a step further and makes Shchusev's later design seem laboured and unoriginal. Commissioned by the railway tycoon Savva Mamontov (who was arrested in 1899 for financial irregularities in the building of this railway but was later declared innocent), it celebrates the first line to northern Russia, the 'real' Russia. From here the Trans-Siberian starts its journey to Vladivostock and China. With the oversized, steeply pitched roof defining the entrance and tent-shaped towers at either end, Shekhtel lightly transposes elements of northern, wooden architecture into a wonderfully attractive, but entirely functional building. The colourful ceramics were made at Mamontov's famous arts and crafts centre at Abramtsevo near Moscow.

*91. The neo-Russian Tretyakov Passageway (1871), was a rare exception of a new gate into Kitai-gorod, east of the Kremlin, which was surrounded by a wall with few gateways until the 1930s. Nowadays the wall has gone and Kitai-gorod is exposed to all.*

*90. The Kazan railway station, was built (1913-26) by Alexei Shchusev as the terminal for the service to Central Asia. It belongs to the railway boom of the turn of the century and consciously imitates the Kremlin at Kazan.*

# ART NOUVEAU AND OLD BELIEVERS

The Yaroslavl Railway Station is an intriguing amalgamation of a romantic view of old Russia with the extravagant flowing lines of Art Nouveau, which in Moscow found a warm welcome. The success of this style was connected to the rise of the new merchant class and the links many of them had with the Old Believer sects. It seems paradoxical, but traditional strict Old Believers were attracted to the revolutionary, almost voluptuous, and always original lines of Art Nouveau. By the third generation, hard-working families had made their money and the narrow world of their business had begun to pall. These new generations of the now established families broke the pattern, becoming fanatical and highly successful art collectors, patrons of the arts or philanthropists on a large scale. Their mansions, dotted about Moscow within the Garden Ring, are still astonishing for their originality and *joie de vivre*.

**Two Shekhtel Mansions** Fyodor Shekhtel, whose family came to Russia from Germany under Catherine, was the most prolific and talented of the architects of the brief Art Nouveau period. With his remarkable energy he is responsible for over fifty buildings in the city, only some of which are in the Art Nouveau style. The most outstanding of the private houses of this period is his masterpiece, the mansion for Stepan Ryabushinsky at Nikitsky Gate, facing the large Church of the Ascension. Roofs are of varying heights; every window, some the shape of keyholes, is different. Each doorway, too, is handled in an individual manner. Under the overhanging roof, a broad mosaic frieze of dying irises is occasionally pierced by upper windows framed in gold leaf. The house is finished in glazed brick and pink stucco. The rooms are grouped around a fantastic staircase of warm Italian

92. *This mansion, housing the Institute of Social Hygiene, was built in 1888 for a silk merchant, who was one of the first Moscow citizens to have a specially built garage.*

93. *Kuznetsky Most, one of Moscow's principal shopping streets before the Revolution, is now known for its many bookshops.*

94. *The statue of Alexander Pushkin, Russia's greatest poet, is always strewn with flowers. It was unveiled in 1880 in a special ceremony at which Dostoevsky and Turgenev expressed their feelings of Russian nationalism.*

limestone which snakes and twists its way upward, the holes in the balustrade resembling kneaded dough. The theme of water dominates: waves in the parquet floors, drops in the stained glass windows, an undersea kingdom in the ceiling painting and plaster work. Even the lamp in the newel post resembles stalactites.

Stepan Ryabushinsky, was one of eight brothers who made a distinct contribution to Moscow life at the beginning of the century, a second-generation Old Believer family. In the tower is an amazing survival

of the original, secret chapel, built before the ban on Old Believer churches was rescinded. What would appear to be a contradiction between conservative Old Believers and the avant-garde of the Art Nouveau style is here wonderfully resolved. Stepan provided yet another vivid contrast in that he was a serious collector of icons: his enviable collection is now in the Tretyakov Gallery. But it is not so hard to imagine them displayed in that odd house, their strong primary colours complementing the exuberant modern design.

In 1931, the writer Maxim Gorky, who although never a Party member sympathised with the Bolsheviks, returned to live in Russia and was granted the use of this mansion. He complained that he felt very uncomfortable in such a luxurious and exotic house. While living there he received George Bernard Shaw, Romain Roland and Stalin himself. He died in 1936, possibly poisoned by order of Stalin.

Another mansion by Shekhtel, built almost at the same time as the Ryabushinsky house, in Shtatniy (Kropotkinsky) Lane, is entirely different in concept. Whereas the Ryabushinsky house always observes domestic proportions, the house for the daughter of a local factory owner, Alexandra Derozhinskaya, is on a much grander scale. Again of glazed brick, this time a soft green, with a rather plain exterior, it is dominated by a large central room resembling a medieval hall with a vast fireplace and panelling and one huge window overlooking the front garden. It is as if intended for giants. The other rooms are less gargantuan and there are many enticing details: the sideboard in the dining room, the fireplaces and gallery for books in the study, the ceiling light-fittings and even the remarkable door handles are all from the architect's imagination. The wonderfully intricate triangle within triangles in the design of the iron railing was repeated in the original upholstery, also designed by Shekhtel, which has not survived. The house is now the Embassy of Australia.

The western side of Moscow between the Boulevard and the Garden Ring became very fashionable in the early years of this century for *nouveau riche* and gentry alike. A large private house built in 1903 on the Povarskaya was commissioned by another industrialist Mindovsky. It is among the best work of the remarkable Lev Kekushev, who also enjoyed the freedom of design provided by Art Nouveau. The house is more sensual, more sculptural, than Shekhtel's houses; the bay and balcony and round corner are defined by the rippling eaves. It is currently used by the New Zealand Embassy and much of the interior design remains.

**Two Churches** After 1905, when the ban was lifted on the building of Old Believer churches, several were built in Moscow in the Art Nouveau style. There are no Orthodox churches in this style. In eastern Moscow, on Gavrikov Lane, the Uspensky-Pokrovsky Community of Old Believers in 1911 built a church designed by Ilya Bondarenko using Novgorod church architecture as inspiration but exaggerating its features. It has been long used as a sports centre.

As you drive down Tverskaya towards the centre, across the railway bridge opposite the Belorussian Station, you are greeted by the huge white edifice of **St Nicholas** (*Nikoly*). The church has a monumental appearance: a square block relieved only here and there by vertical fenestration. It was the last church to be started in Moscow before the

*96. Russian school children study a sculpture in the New Tretyakov Gallery of Russian art. The old gallery has been rebuilt and expanded to accommodate the large collection of Russian art started by Pavel Tretyakov.*

Revolution and, interrupted by war and revolution, was not finished until 1920, when it functioned as an Old Believer church for some years before being closed. It is now being returned to its original owners.

# PUBLIC BUILDINGS

One of the most remarkable figures in the early years of this century was Ivan Sytin, who came to Moscow as an unlettered peasant boy, got a job selling books on a stall, and learned to read and write. Then, with remarkable energy, he set up his own book stall and in time embarked upon the publishing of cheap editions of the classics, encyclopaedias and the like. He rightly foresaw that the spread of education, which was then proceeding rapidly in the villages, would make for a new reading public. In 1907 his fine Art Nouveau building on Tverskaya, designed by Adolf Erichson, with its flower mosaics, scrolls and varied windows, was ready for his offices, printing house and penthouse apartment on the fifth floor. After the Revolution it was taken over by *Pravda* and Sytin was dispossessed. However, he was kept on as consultant to the publishing industry and even given a pension in 1928 — an unusual event for a former capitalist in Soviet Russia. In the 1970s the building was moved some fifty metres to make way for the new *Izvestiya* building. It now houses a less sympathetic car firm, Trinity.

**Experimental Nursery School** Among burgeoning factories in the unfashionable area north of the Garden Ring is a fantastic building: Stanislav Shatsky's experimental institution for pre-school children. With its tower and strangely shaped bulbous bays it looks outlandish, especially in modern Moscow. Built in 1907 to encourage poor children

*97. The Pushkin Gallery of Fine Art displays paintings and sculpture from western countries in a classical building by Roman Klein that was opened by Nicholas II in 1912.*

in the elementary sciences, arts and community spirit, it was equipped with an observatory and special laboratories. Paid for by public subscription, it is an example of the energy with which educational problems were beginning to be treated in those pre-Revolutionary days. It is the only building by the imaginative architect Alexander Zelenko to survive.

**Medvednikov Poor-house** The merchant or business community was very active before the First World War in establishing charity organisations. Moscow by this time had begun to acquire the infrastructure needed for a modern city: sewers, indoor plumbing, public transport in the form of trams. Even telephone lines had been set up by a private Danish firm. By 1916 there were 55,000 subscribers, not a small number compared to other major cities of this period. It was the merchants who began to provide a measure of social security for the less well-off sector of society. Many peasants had come to the big city to seek their fortune and many were working for harsh masters in the proliferating small industries. And many were unable to find work. The richer merchants, feeling it was their duty to provide amenities for these numerous people, set up hospitals, poor-houses and schools, and even subsidised housing on a considerable scale.

One such was the Medvednikov Poor-house in south Moscow, not far from the Garden Ring and almost directly opposite the tsar's Alexandra Palace. Its dynamic design was by Sergei Solovyov, another original architect, in a neo-Russian, modern style with borrowings from Novgorod and Pskov architecture.

**The Metropole** Many luxurious new hotels were built in Moscow at the beginning of the century, especially by insurance companies, which increasingly prospered as Moscow became the financial centre of the

Empire. Perhaps the finest was the Metropole, erected in the central Theatre Square. It was intended as Moscow's first hotel with *de luxe* rooms, premises let to businesses, and even highly comfortable flats. Its odd position, set against the wall of Kitai-gorod, dictated its plan. The St Petersburg Insurance Society, the owners, preferred the plan submitted by Kekushev, but Savva Mamontov, of the arts and crafts group at Abramtsevo and head of the jury, ultimately decided in favour of William Walcot's design, which allowed more possibilities for artistic embellishment. Walcot, born in Russia of a Russian mother and English father (he emigrated to England in 1906) has provided an unusual façade. Balconies divide the building horizontally — above is a frieze of figures by Moscow's greatest sculptor of the age, Nikolai Andreyev. The slogan in coloured tiles 'Proletariat of all Countries Unite' was added after the Revolution in place of a quotation from Nietzsche. Of the upper panels, the central northern one, by Mikhail Vrubel, depicts the *Princesse Lointaine* by Edmund Rostand. Other mosaics are by Golovin. A great glass dome provides the roofing for the main restaurant.

After the Revolution the Metropole was used as the House of Soviets for offices and meetings, but at the end of the 1920s it became a hotel again. In the mid-Eighties it closed for lengthy reconstruction, carried out by Finnish contractors on behalf of Intourist. Happily, the interiors were intelligently restored, some to the original Art Nouveau style, and the great dining room and tea room on the top floor are once again looking as they did about 1910.

**Apartment Blocks** As the population increased, accommodation in the centre grew scarce; not everyone could afford to build idiosyncratic mansions. Apartment buildings for the middle classes, the bourgeoisie, began to spring up all over Moscow from the turn of the century to 1917. They contained large apartments, sometimes seven large rooms, with modern amenities such as bathrooms, rooms for the servants, even in one case underground parking.

After the Revolution these apartments were appropriated and divided, and the former inhabitants allowed only a corner. They have remained communal flats until the present day, although recently foreign and Russian firms have begun to take them over. Many were designed in the flamboyant style of Art Nouveau, such as the **Chizhikov apartment block** on the Kudrinskaya Garden Ring, built in 1901. Such blocks are generally in poor condition inside, but at least the staircase usually survives.

One of the best examples is the **Makayev apartment block** in Podsosensky Lane near the Boulevard, east of the Kremlin. Built in 1903 by the architect Prince George Makayev and now in lamentable condition (it lost a balcony only recently), it occupies a corner site that accommodates a tower on which long-stemmed flowers climb the whole height of the building.

Another fine block with the usual five storeys is the **Isakov building** on Prechistenka, designed in 1906 by Kekushev. The curved bays at either end and recessed central section with wrought-iron balconies give it a languorous quality. The overhanging eaves of the roof follow this curving movement brilliantly; in the pediment there is a sculpture of two female figures flanking a round window. Happily, the original glazing is not lost.

It is easy to miss the 1903 **Sokol apartment house**, designed by Ivan Mashkov on narrow, crowded Kuznetsky Most. But look upwards and see curved bays in the centre and at the ends, and the great tiled panel celebrating a falcon flying in the blue, blue sky.

# RETURN TO NEO-CLASSICISM

The failure of the 1905 Revolution to achieve lasting reforms was decisive in determining the second, 1917 Revolution. The parliament conceded by Nicholas II was able to operate as a genuine legislative body for only a very short period; by 1907 it had lost power and the Emperor was able to dismiss it without serious repercussion. From then on Nicholas and his advisors, who came and went with alarming speed, held all the strings. The role of the Tsaritsa, born a German princess, further alienated the court from the Russian people, especially her relationship with the eccentric monk, Grigory Rasputin, who seemed able to control her son's haemophilia.

Political developments are closely reflected in architectural preferences of a particular age. It is true that Art Nouveau and the neo-Russian styles were dying a natural death by the end of the twentieth century's first decade, but the triumph of conservative forces in the political sphere helped decide the new course in building styles. By 1910 new buildings in Moscow had turned to the safer domain of classical forms, so closely associated with the idealised period of Pushkin and the Golden Age in the early nineteenth century. For the state, classical forms automatically spelt reassurance.

**Comfortable Houses**  One of the prettiest houses of this period — and the style does lend itself remarkably well to small, individual mansions — is the mansion built in 1913 for the influential industrialist Nikolai Vtorov, now the residence of the American Ambassador. It is reminiscent of the Russian Empire style, although its interior planning is more freely constructed.

Fyodor Shekhtel, the Art Nouveau architect, also succumbed to the new trends. In 1910 he built for himself a classical house on the Garden Ring that makes use of a portico and sculptural panel similar to the Empire houses, but its asymmetry and free planning are distinctly Shekhtel. Like other members of the bourgeoisie, in 1918 he was obliged to leave this comfortable house and move to a communal flat, where he spent his last years.

An impressive building of this period is the **Tarasov Mansion** (1912), an imitation of Palladio's Thiene Palace in Vicenza, with its severely rusticated exterior in contrast to the charming courtyard and rich interiors. The architect, Ivan Zholtovsky, spent a great deal of time in Italy as a young man, and became imbued with a passion for Italian Renaissance architecture that he transferred to his Moscow buildings. Paradoxically, he later became one of the most successful architects in the Soviet period.

**Pushkin Museum**  The most important of the neo-classical buildings is the Pushkin Museum of Fine Art (originally the Alexander III Museum), completed in 1912. It was commissioned from the Moscow architect Roman Klein, assisted by Pyotr Boitsev, as a museum to house the classical plaster casts of Moscow University.

Professor Ivan Tsvetaev, a specialist in Roman literature and art history, personally pursued the idea of the museum, travelling throughout Europe to make copies of sculpture and following up every possibility of obtaining donations. Nechaev-Maltsev, the owner of the Gusev porcelain works, proved to be the most generous supporter and made it possible for the museum to be completed.

98. *Russian medieval motifs,
which became popular at the
end of the 19th century, are evident in this colourful mansion
built for the Igumov family
(1893), by the Yaroslavl architect, Nikolai Pozdeyev, now the
residence of the French ambassador.*

Its Ionic portico and frieze, a copy of the Erechtheum portico in the Parthenon, leads into the low-slung building with a magnificent staircase by Zholtovsky. This leads up to a charming basilica-type room, where concerts and special exhibitions are held, and a long hall where Greek sculpture is displayed to great effect. Tsvetaev's daughter, the tragic poetess Marina Tsvetaeva, has left a charming poem describing the opening of the museum attended by the Tsar and his daughters: 'a cloud of white butterflies' on a perfect May day. Professor Tsvetaev died a year after his life's work was completed.

After the Revolution, the museum began to house paintings taken from the private collections of the prescient merchants such as Sergei Shchukin and Ivan Morozov. It is now better known for its magnificent west European paintings than its sculptures, and particularly for its art of the impressionist and post-impressionist periods, including works by Picasso, Monet, Renoir, Van Gogh, Cezanne, Gauguin, and Matisse. It has also acquired, mostly from private collections, works by Botticelli, Cranach the Elder, Rembrandt, Van Dyck, Goya, Poussin, Boucher and Fragonard. In addition, it has an impressive Egyptian collection, assembled in the nineteenth century by V. Golenishchev.

# THE SOVIET PERIOD

*99. The railway line from
Moscow to Archangelsk was an
important factor in opening up
the Russian north. The highly
original station by Fyodor
Shekhtel (1904) reflects the
sense of adventure. The owner,
Savva Mamontov, used his arts
and crafts centre at Abramtsevo
for the tile work, such as the
giant strawberries. Note the
hammer and sickle which
replaced the railway logo.*

Russia's entry into the First World War was greeted with patriotic enthusiasm by the population of Moscow. Demonstrations broke out against German firms such as the music shop selling Bechstein pianos.

*101. In appearance a mansion of the post-1812 classical period, it was built a century later (1913) for Nikolai Vtorov, the Siberian manufacturer. Now the residence of the American ambassador, it is popularly known as Spaso House.*

But by 1915-16 the Russian army was in retreat, casualties were heavy, the army was poorly outfitted, and there were many desertions. Disillusion set in and the political situation became more unstable. By February 1917 confidence in the Tsar had clearly evaporated, and after demonstrations in Petrograd (St Petersburg), he was obliged to abdicate. A Provisional Government under Kerensky took power and the ill-fated Tsar Nicholas II and his family were taken to Siberia, first to Tobolsk and eventually to Yekaterinburg where, in July 1918, they were executed.

Meanwhile, the Bolsheviks, together with their allies the Mensheviks, set up a Workers' Soviet in the Tauride Palace, which exercised dual power alongside the Provisional Government. Although the Bolshevik fortunes ebbed during the July 1917 days, when they attempted a premature coup, by the autumn their star was in the ascendant and in October they were strong enough to stage the final, successful coup.

Whereas the Revolution in Petrograd was bloodless, in Moscow desperate fighting broke out in the streets and went on for a week. White troops loyal to Kerensky held the Kremlin until it was stormed a week later and taken by Red forces. About two hundred and fifty people died in Moscow during the Revolution and many buildings in the centre were damaged, including the Assumption Cathedral in the Kremlin.

Early in 1918 the new government decided to move to Moscow as the Germans, with no-one to oppose them, were moving closer to Petrograd. In March, after a brief stay in the National Hotel, Lenin, his wife, Krupskaya, and other leading figures moved into the Kremlin, where Lenin took up offices in the old Senate. The old Kremlin walls, silent for two hundred years, became alive again with this influx of peo-

*100. Apartments for the well-to-do sprang up all over Moscow at the turn of the century. This one in restrained Art Nouveau style was built by A. Chizhikov (1901). Three more stories were discreetly added in 1940, a common device to increase housing.*

ple. But a cruel civil war broke out beyond Moscow and Petrograd which continued for three years, bringing in its wake dreadful famine and fuel shortages. Moscow became run-down, people queued desperately for food. The fine apartments of the middle classes were confiscated and given to the less well-off, with the former owner lucky to keep even a corner for himself. From Russia as a whole over one million people, mostly from the nobility and bourgeoisie, emigrated.

Yet by 1921 the civil war was virtually over, the stringent economic policies of War Communism — forced grain requisitions and tight state control of the economy — were abandoned, and the New Economic Policy was inaugurated by Lenin. Under this plan, some aspects of a market economy were restored in order to give the country time to recover. The government kept control only of the 'commanding heights' of the economy. The relative liberal period of the NEP lasted until 1928, its demise coinciding with Stalin's victory over his chief rivals. During this first decade of Soviet power, the arts, including architecture, flourished under official encouragement despite the difficulties.

## THE AVANT-GARDE

Many of the avant-garde artists of the new generation welcomed the Revolution with open arms. It reinforced their ideals and they thought the new regime would be more sympathetic to their art than the conservative tsarist government. Artists of the calibre of Rodchenko, Chagall, Malevich, Tatlin, Gabo, and Lissitsky set up free studios and undertook commissions for the Bolsheviks, encouraged by Anatoly Lunarcharsky, the Minister for Enlightenment. Architecture, too, attracted young, relatively new talent. Artists, sculptors and architects met in the former School of Painting, Sculpture and Architecture, now the Vkhutemas, where the three arts interwove and inspired one another.

These were heady days. The Bolshevik regime needed new sorts of buildings — workers' clubs, newspaper offices, exhibition pavilions — dramatic and visual propaganda for its stated goal of the establishment of the utopian workers' state. Architectural competitions for idealised buildings became the order of the day. One for the Palace of Industry envisaged the whole of Red Square and much of Kitai-gorod being razed to erect a gigantic ministry. The entry of the visionary architect, Leonidov, was a fifty-storey building in the shape of a factory chimney. Fortunately, the designs for the Palace of Industry remained on the drawing boards, but the south part of Kitai-gorod was demolished nevertheless. The ugly building site remained vacant for decades until, in the 1960s, the unattractive square block that is the Rossiya Hotel came into being — the largest in Europe with the reputation of the most inefficient.

The new avant-garde style of art and architecture, loosely known as constructivism, developed out of the more rational modern style that had been evolving before the Revolution. It was essentially the employment of bare geometrical forms, both inside and out, eschewing all decoration. Improved building materials were used creatively — particularly reinforced concrete and glass. The style remained dominant until the late Twenties. The buildings erected in Moscow in this period are extraordinarily daring and modern, surpassing anything elsewhere, including even the Bauhaus designs in Germany.

ЛЕНИН

*103. Lenin shared his last resting place with Stalin from the latter's death in 1953 until 1961, when his body was secretly removed and buried behind, by the Kremlin wall. Although Lenin still occupies the mausoleum, there are rumours he may have to leave.*

**Melnikov** Konstantin Melnikov, aged twenty-seven at the time of the Revolution, was one of the most prolific and imaginative architects of this period. Already in 1916 he had designed the main building for the AMO (now ZIL) car factory. In 1925 he was selected to design the Soviet pavilion for the Paris Exhibition of Decorative Arts. He executed the task brilliantly. With its interior photomontage by Alexander Rodchenko and notes by Vladimir Mayakovsky, it was a concord of the arts and won the Grand Prix.

In Moscow Melnikov began building workers' clubs which would be attached to particular factories and thus bring culture directly to the working class. His masterpiece is the Rusakov Club (1928) for municipal employees in eastern Moscow, beyond the three railway stations. It an impressive sight: three large cantilevered sections hang from the first floor, divided by vertical slabs of long fenestration. Within these sections is the seating of the ambitious auditorium, which can be divided by mechanical partitions into three smaller theatres or left as one large hall.

Melnikov's own house, which he built in 1929, was equally daring. Using brick, wood and plaster, it is composed of two enmeshed cylinders linked by a staircase where they intersect, producing wedge-shaped rooms on the ground floor, bedrooms on the first floor, divided only by partitions, and spacious studios. The top floor is lit by hexagonal windows which, placed at intervals throughout the brick walls, can be covered up or released as desired to produce varied patterns.

The atmosphere changed with the rise of Stalin, and in the Thirties Melnikov was heavily criticised for formalism. From then on he never built again, though he entered many competitions. He died a bitter man in 1974. Ironically, shortly afterwards his work began to be recognised and appreciated, and has now taken its proper place in the history of architecture. The unique house, the only one in Soviet Moscow designed and lived in by the architect, has remained in his family.

**Zuyev Club**   Another impressive workers' club, erected for the employees of the department of municipal economy in 1929, was designed by the romantic Ilya Golosov. Its intriguing design consists of a great glass cylinder enclosing the staircase, intended to be reminiscent of an elevator, while the long concrete form extending from the cylinder is like a factory. Like other workers' clubs of this period, it is now used as a more general cinema cum social club for the local district.

**The Media**   The Bolsheviks, now in absolute control of mass media, needed specially designed newspaper buildings. The old block of the Izvestiya building on Pushkin Square was built in 1927 by Grigory Barkhin. The square extruding balconies, common in buildings of this period, on one side, the splendid large clock with its square face — the same size as the round portal-like windows on the upper floor, and the sign for Izvestiya (originally in giant lettering) break up the otherwise too regular façade. Its excellent design contrasts sharply with the modern wing put up in the mid-Seventies.

**Living Space**   Behind the old building of the American Embassy on the Garden Ring Road is one of the symbols of the Twenties: apartments for the Commissariat of Finance (Narkomfin) built by Moishe Ginsburg (the theoretician of constructivism), and now sadly reduced to semi-dereliction. It was here that he created the famous F-type apartment on two levels in the hope they would not become communal (they did). And on the then southern border of Moscow, near the Donskoi Monastery, a hostel for students of the textile institute was built by Ivan Nikolaev (1930), consisting of curves and rectangles incorporating two blocks, one of eight storeys with over a thousand rooms, and a linked three-storey building for dining, sport and library facilities. It is still a hostel.

**Office Blocks**   The great Swiss architect Le Corbusier also participated in the period of avant-garde construction in Moscow. He won the competition for the office block for the Centrosoyuz, the Central Union of Consumer Societies, built in place of a demolished church on Kirov (Myasnitskaya) Street. Eight stories high and faced in pink tufa stone, it is designed in the form of an H on *piloti* (stilts), with horizontal fenestration. The main entrance is on Novokirovskaya Street, a new avenue not built until the 1970s. It is an assertively modern building. When it was completed in 1936, Le Corbusier received scant praise in the Soviet press, which had by then turned totally against modern architecture. In a complete about face, the monumental classical became the accepted style.

On the north-east side of the Garden Ring is the Ministry of Agriculture building, constructed (1928-33) for the then Commissariat of Agriculture by the well-known pre-Revolutionary architect Alexei Shchusev. It proves his ability to design in almost any style he chose, for here are the essentials of the avant-garde of the Twenties: horizontal fenestration, on a concrete and steel frame, an attractive glazed circular tower-like bay on the corner, and even the square clock encountered in the *Izvestiya* building. All is finished in pink render, nowadays rather

*104. The huge Stalinist Gothic apartment block (1952) broods over the 1764 Foundling Home, miniature in comparison, although in its time it was the largest building in Europe.*

dusty. This building seems to have been the model for many other office blocks of the period encountered in Moscow. Shchusev's work is a far cry from his Art Nouveau church in the Martha-Mary Community.

**Lenin Mausoleum**  Shchusev was also the architect of the most important cult building of the period. After a series of disabling strokes in 1923, Lenin died in the bitterly cold January of 1924. His colleagues decided to preserve his body and make a cult of his memory, in spite of his express wish, according to his widow, to be buried in his home town, Samara. Shchusev designed the first, temporary wooden structure to house his remains, erected in a matter of days in temperatues of minus 30 degrees. The position chosen, in front of the Senate tower, was where Lenin liked to address the crowds on the anniversaries of the Revolution and on May Day. It was to become the traditional place for the leadership to view the military parades and popular demonstrations that were such a feature of the Soviet era.

A competition was held to find the best design for the permanent mausoleum. Melnikov and Shekhtel submitted plans, but Shchusev won the contest. His design of a pared-down classical tribunal, under which the body lay in state in a tomb of black labradorite stone and pink granite, is restrained and tactful. The whole structure does not reach the top of the Kremlin wall and fits almost unobtrusively into the square. At the same time Red Square was altered in other less acceptable ways. The lovely Iberian Gate (*Iverskye Vorota*) between the History and Lenin Museums was demolished (even the tsar saluted the icon of Our Lady of Iberia in the chapel when he passed through the gate). The splendid Cathedral of the Kazan Virgin, which stood on the corner of Nikolskaya opposite the History Museum and GUM, was also demolished at this

*105. Mikhail Lomonosov, founder of the University of Moscow, stands in front of the 36-storey building (1953) on Sparrow Hills. It is the most impressive of the seven high-rise structures that circle Moscow's old centre.*

*107. The upper parts of the high-rise tower blocks are strongly reminiscent of Gothic cathedrals. The inhabitants of this apartment block have wonderful views of the Kremlin, the Yauza and Moskva Rivers, and the district of Zamoskvoreche.*

*106. The Ministry of Defence building (1943-45) in Soviet monumental style. It was designed by Mikhail Posokhin, city architect for over 20 years, using as its foundation the 18th-century Alexander Cadet Academy.*

time, and the statue of Minin and Pozharsky moved back away from the centre of the square. It is only by a miracle that St Basil's was not also removed to allow the free flow of columns of military equipment during parades. Thus, the reorganised Red Square, deprived of some of its most historic buildings, became a political stage and a powerful symbol of the Soviet regime.

## STALIN RECONSTRUCTION

By 1929 Stalin had outwitted and defeated his rivals. The most powerful of them, Trotsky, was exiled in 1929, eventually to be murdered in Mexico by Soviet agents. From this time the country was irrevocably set on a different and fatal course. Stalin inaugurated the first five-year plan in 1929 and effectively put an end to the operation of market forces under the NEP. He began a drive for rapid industrialisation and the forced collectivisation of agriculture. The peasants slaughtered their livestock rather than submit and in 1933 there was a terrible famine in the Ukraine and Russia as even the seed grain was confiscated to feed the cities. Millions died then, millions more were deported as *kulaks* ('rich peasants'); the countryside and Soviet agriculture never recovered from this man-made disaster. With the expansion of the factories, cities grew apace and many new ones were founded. Moscow's population expanded rapidly in the Thirties as the capital and the region around it were organised as the central industrial zone. By 1939 it had over four million inhabitants, exceeding by one million the population of Leningrad, as St Petersburg was called after Lenin's death.

A sweeping plan for the reconstruction of Moscow was adopted in 1935, envisaging new avenues and the building of the metro. Meanwhile,

Stalin kept his hold on power by eliminating anyone he thought might threaten him, including all Lenin's closest colleagues. The period of the dreaded purges began in 1934, when the popular First Party Secretary in Leningrad, Sergei Kirov, was assassinated (as is now known) by order of Stalin himself. This inaugurated a fierce purge of party officials involving arrests, imprisonment and executions. But this was only the beginning. In 1937, the worst year, millions of people were arrested, shot or sent to the notorious Siberian camps by the secret police, the NKVD. The arrests only stopped — momentarily — with the outbreak of World War II. Moscow in the Thirties and Forties must be considered against this dreadful political background.

Moscow's architecture was also affected by the rise of Joseph Stalin. The experimental, avant-garde architecture of the Twenties gave way to the state-sponsored revival of the perennial style, neo-classicism. But it was neo-classicism on a monumental scale never experienced before. It is, however, piquant that some of the same architects involved in constructivist and earlier styles adapted quite easily to the Soviet grandomania.

**Lenin Library** The largest library in the world, now renamed the Russian State Library, was founded after the Revolution on the basis of the already large library of the Rumyantsev Museum. The new library was considerably enlarged by the requisitioning of private libraries, of which there were many in Moscow before the Revolution. In the late Twenties, a competition for the design of the library building was held, which the avant-garde architects entered, but it was won by Vladimir Shchuko and Vladimir Gelfreikh, favoured architects of the Stalin period. Begun in 1928, the library is a curious amalgam of austerity and extravagance, illustrating the increasing preference for classical devices. The portico of the main building is of plain square black granite columns in the 'proletarian classical' style. Later a bold frieze was added, and along the street line statues of classical figures were placed on the roof. Medallions, too, appeared on the walls, portraying scientific and literary figures — it seems that nearly every Soviet sculptor was given a commission for this building. Within are marble stairs and columns, plastered ceilings and fine spacious reading rooms.

Almost certainly the monumental style of the library was influenced by the nearby building site for the gigantic Palace of Soviets on the place of the demolished monument to the 1812 victory over Napoleon, the Cathedral of Christ the Redeemer (*Khrista Spasitelya*). The tiered palace was to have been the tallest building in the world, with endless columns and other classical attributes, the epitome of the Stalinist monumental style, crowned by a 75-metre-high statue of Lenin. It is significant that proposed designs for the palace by Le Corbusier and Melnikov were not successful. However, in the end it never got above ground-floor level: there were severe problems with river seepage, and construction was suspended when the war began in 1941 and never resumed. Today the Moskva swimming pool occupies the site, although there is a popular campaign to rebuild the vast, cumbersome and undeniably ugly cathedral.

**New Avenues** The 1935 Plan envisaged the construction of many new avenues, one of which, the New Arbat, was not built until the early Sixties. Cutting a merciless swathe through one of Moscow's most lovely and historic districts, its main purpose was simply to allow Soviet leaders

*108. The gilded Fountain of the Friendship of the Peoples, located in the Exhibition of Economic Achievements.*

*109. A Kosmos rocket in the Space Pavilion of the Economic Achievements Exhibition.*

to get to their dachas quickly. The plan also included the widening of the major radial road, Tverskaya, then named Gorky Street. A winding, narrow street until the second half of the Thirties, it was more than doubled in width and straightened in an amazing engineering operation. Many old houses and churches were demolished, but a few buildings were literally lifted and moved back, some as much as 20 metres.

One of the buildings that was moved was the former palace of the governor-general in Moscow, a classical mansion built by Matvei Kazakov in 1782. (In 1917 it was the headquarters of the Provisional Government and then, of the Soviet of Workers' Deputies, which helped organise the Revolution in Moscow.) In 1939 it was moved 14 metres back in order to widen the road. In the Forties, in the middle of the war, it was drastically remodelled: a huge Soviet arch and two additional floors completely transformed the Kazakov building into something more in keeping with the Soviet monumental style. At the same time, along the widened artery heavy new apartment buildings with shops on the ground floor were constructed in place of the demolished buildings. On the east side, Nos 4 and 6 with motifs of shafts of wheat in low relief were designed by Arkady Mordvinov, who is also responsible for the Italianate grey blocks further up on the west side. Access to the still charming side streets were through immense Soviet-style arches.

A few of the architects of the classical style before the Revolution came back into their own when the avant-garde tide receded. Ivan Zholtovsky built a nearly perfect Renaissance building on the Mokhovaya (Prospekt Marxa) in 1934. With its giant orders it is typical of Soviet Moscow, yet it matches the classical style of the Old University next door. Inside is a delightful courtyard that would not be out of place

*110. Yuri Gagarin was the first person to travel into space, in 1961. This stylised statue of him in cosmonaut's suit erected in the early 1980s was instantly dubbed 'action man' by Moscow's foreign residents.*

*111. Statue of Yury Dolgoruky, founder of Moscow, erected in 1947 to mark the 800th anniversary of the city.*

112. The colonnade of the Borodino Bridge (architect Roman Klein) was erected in 1912 to mark the entrance to the city and the centenary of the battle of Borodino and the defeat of Napoleon.

113. The Arbat, Moscow's most famous street, became in 1985 its first pedestrian walkway. Many writers, artists and scientists lived on this street and it figures prominently in Soviet literature, for example, Rybakov's 'Children of the Arbat'.

in Siena or Verona. For some twenty years, until the early Fifties, this building served as the United States Embassy.

**Soviet Jokes** Some Stalinist buildings, sombre and grey as they may seem, on closer inspection have a humorous aspect. One such is the lugubrious Moskva Hotel, built in the very heart of Moscow just outside Red Square. Here Shchusev's career nearly came unstuck. For the first new Soviet hotel in Moscow the approval of Stalin had to be sought, as in the case of all major buildings in the capital. Shchusev included two variants of the design for the wings on a plan that was handed to the great leader without explanation. Stalin put his signature on the whole plan without indicating which variant he preferred. Poor Shchusev did not dare ask him to look at the scheme again and so in desperation built the hotel with both variants. The wings on either side of the central colonnade thus differ wildly from each other.

Another of these macabre jokes has to do with the huge Red Army Theatre, built by Alabyan next to the House of Officers (the former Catherine Institute for Daughters of the Nobility) in 1940. It is in the shape of a Red Army five-pointed star lined with columns all the way around. The surfeit of columns and the strange shape are not conducive to the needs of a theatre. Khrushchev, during one of his public tirades against modern art, declared that the design was hopelessly impractical and in any case could only be appreciated from a helicopter.

**Engineering** Perhaps the most attractive of the neo-classical buildings of the Stalin era is the tall slim tower of the Northern River Station on the Khimki reservoir, constructed at the same time as the 126-kilometre Moscow-Volga canal. One of the engineering feats of the

119

Thirties, the canals that link Moscow and the five seas of the Caspian, Azov, Black, Baltic and White, were built with great human suffering.

Other, more positive, architectural achievements of the Stalin era in Moscow are also in the form of engineering: the strengthening of the river embankments, the building of new bridges, and the construction of the magnificent metro. The last is a real monument to the era. Each station was to be different from the others and designed in an original manner, with no expense spared.

The early lines opened in 1935 were the most successful in this respect. The red marble of Krasnyye Vorota (Ukhtomsky's 1757 Red Gate in honour of Elizabeth's coronation which was pulled down before the metro opened) on the Mayakovskaya line, with its wonderful stone and metal arched hall, provided spacious and palatial interiors for a public living in extremely poor and crowded housing. In the early Fifties the luxuriously appointed and excessively decorated Circle line was built. The Komsomolskaya Station, serving the three railway stations, is the most extreme, with its heavy gilt and its ceiling mosaics depicting leaders on the mausoleum in Red Square. The figures had to be periodically changed as leaders fell out of favour.

**Stalinist Gothic**  Stalin ruled for over a quarter of a century and died in his bed like his mentor, Ivan the Terrible. The last and in some ways most memorable architectural expression of his era was the construction of the high-rise wedding-cake towers placed at strategic points around the city. Most were located outside or on the Garden Ring. The Ukraine Hotel with its tiered form of 36 storeys dominates the reach of the Moskva River which it overlooks. It is encrusted with towers and baubles on its roof line, in the manner of Gothic churches. Indeed, the comparison with medieval Gothic cathedrals is not inappropriate. From a distance these seven tall buildings look most impressive.

The best of the towers is the New University in the Sparrow (Lenin) Hills, completed in 1953 by Lev Rudnev, which stands on comparatively empty land overlooking the river and the city from its highest point. Here, the wings and main block of 36 floors with its tall spire exude a kind of serenity. As most of the twenty thousand or so students of the University live in the enormous wings of the main block, and many facilities, even shops, are on hand, the building is a small city in itself.

## UTILITARIAN ARCHITECTURE

When Stalin died in 1953, his regime did not die with him, but there was a limited reaction against the harshness of his reign. Beria, his notorious policeman, was arrested a few months later and shot without trial in December 1953. The new leadership with Malenkov at its head set out to improve relations with the West and lessen Cold War tensions that had become unbearable. Khrushchev then came to the fore, denounced the abuses of Stalinism and the cult of personality at the 20th Party Congress in 1956, and made tentative efforts to liberalise the political system and reform the economy.

**Krushchev and High Rise**  Khrushchev also intervened arbitrarily in the field of city planning. In 1955 he ordered a halt to the grand buildings still being put up in the expensive classical style. There were to be no baubles. Instead, to tackle the housing problem, which had reached horrendous levels — families of ten living in one room were common — he set underway a huge building programme in the new areas of Moscow's vastly extended frontiers, with the proclaimed aim of providing every family with a self-contained flat. That aim has still not been realised, but the result of his ill-conceived housing programme is that most people in Moscow now live in soulless 'micro districts'. At first Khrushchev approved five-storey 'temporary' blocks to relieve the pressure (five storeys so as to avoid installing lifts), which were meant to have a life of only twenty years. Nowadays, those buildings are still standing, shabby and dilapidated, but at least now surrounded by trees and not so bleak as they first appeared. In the Seventies the policy of building new districts was expanded, but with blocks of flats now up to 22 stories high, huge impersonal edifices which make the old five-storey *'Khrushchovy'* (a pun on the word for slums) seem almost human.

Under Khrushchev the international modern came to Moscow. The Palace of Congresses in the Kremlin has already been mentioned. Another outstanding example is the building which until August 1991 housed Comecon (the Council for Mutual Economic Assistance), designed by Posokhin and others and completed in 1970. Its tower of tall curved wings (32 stories) flanking a slim central core looks from afar like sheets of glass astride the river. Comecon was dissolved after the East European revolutions of 1989 and the building was taken over by the Moscow City Council after the August 1991 failed coup.

Khrushchev was ousted in 1964 by a conspiracy among his colleagues in the party leadership, who accused him of foolhardy foreign adventures (such as the Cuban crisis) and erratic internal policies. Leonid Brezhnev came to the fore among the group of successors. Initial hopes of liberalisation and economic reform soon faded and a long period of what was later to be called stagnation set in. Brezhnev's death, at last, in December 1982 was followed by the brief rule first of Andropov and then Chernenko, who were both elderly and sick and died after a year in office. Even the Party leadership began to sense the need for a time of change and reform as the country's economy declined and living standards fell further and further behind the opulent West.

**Perestroika and the White House** In 1985 the young and energetic Gorbachev was elected to succeed Chernenko as party general secretary. He embarked upon a policy of restructuring (*perestroika*) which involved dismantling the 'administrative-command' economic system, and democratisation of the political system, including the encouragement of greater freedom of speech (*glasnost*). The liberalisation he unleashed developed its own momentum, however, eventually leading to the collapse of the USSR and his own resignation.

In contrast to Comecon and situated to its left is the building now known as the White House (*Bely Dom*). Built in 1981 by Chechulin, (the architect of the elaborate Komsomolskaya metro station), as the House of Soviets (government) for the Russian Republics, it is not as impressive as its neighbour; indeed, it looks like an older building. It became world famous in the exhilarating days of August 1991 when the tanks of the hard-line Communists who organised the

coup against Gorbachev rolled into Moscow. Boris Yeltsin hurried to the White House, which he had made his headquarters since winning the elections for the presidency of Russia in June 1991.

People began to gather around the building as soon as it became known that he was there. Eventually, the crowds outside numbered tens of thousands. They spent the nights of 19 and 20 August camped in unseasonably cold and wet weather and, with the ten tanks that had gone over to Yeltsin, waited for the attack from the coup plotters. Fortunately, their nerve had failed and it never came. By the 21 August Yeltsin and his supporters had won, the tanks moved away, Gorbachev was rescued from his Crimean villa, where he had been incarcerated, and the leaders of the coup were arrested.

Moscow, like Russia, is now in a difficult transitional period, testing all the time the limits of the new democracy, feeling its way to an uncertain future. Its architecture is already beginning to reflect the change. Moscow's buildings are unlikely now to avoid influence from the West, particularly with so many foreign firms flocking to open businesses with the Russians and acquiring and restoring some historic Moscow buildings.

Yet it is a blessing that the city, which did not suffer heavy bombardment in the last war, has survived as well as it has. In central Moscow, even the destruction of nearly half its churches since the Revolution still leaves many from the huge number before 1917. What the city really needs now is sympathetic attention to its elderly housing in the city centre, most of which is suffering through lack of maintenance for the last seventy years, and is falling apart.

*115. Moscow has numerous swimming pools and other excellent sports facilities, many constructed for the 1980 Olympics.*

124

*Andrei Rublev. Old Testament Trinity, early 15th century*
*(Tretyakov Gallery)*

*The Kazan Crown of Ivan the Terrible, 1552*
*(Armoury Museum, Kremlin)*

*Ivan Kramskoi. Portrait of Lev Tolstoy, 1873*
*(Tretyakov Gallery)*

*Vasily Perov. Portrait of Fyodor Dostoevsky, 1872*
*(Tretyakov Gallery)*

*Vasily Surikov. Boyarina Morozova, 1887*
*(Tretyakov Gallery)*

*Ivan Kramskoi. The Unknown Lady, 1883*

*Ilya Repin. They Did Not Expect Him, 1884-88*
*(Tretyakov Gallery)*

*Viktor Vasnetsov. Bogatyrs (Warrior Heroes), 1890*
*(Tretyakov Gallery)*

*Alexei Venetsianov. Harvest Time: Summer, 1820s*
*(Tretyakov Gallery)*

*Vasily Tropinin. Portrait of the Artist's Son, c.1818*
*(Tretyakov Gallery)*

*Claude Monet. Luncheon on the Grass, 1866*
*(Pushkin Gallery)*

*Kuzma Petrov-Vodkin. Red Horse Swimming, 1912*
*(Tretyakov Gallery)*

*Sergei Gerasimov. Collective Farm Holiday, 1937*
*(Tretyakov Gallery)*

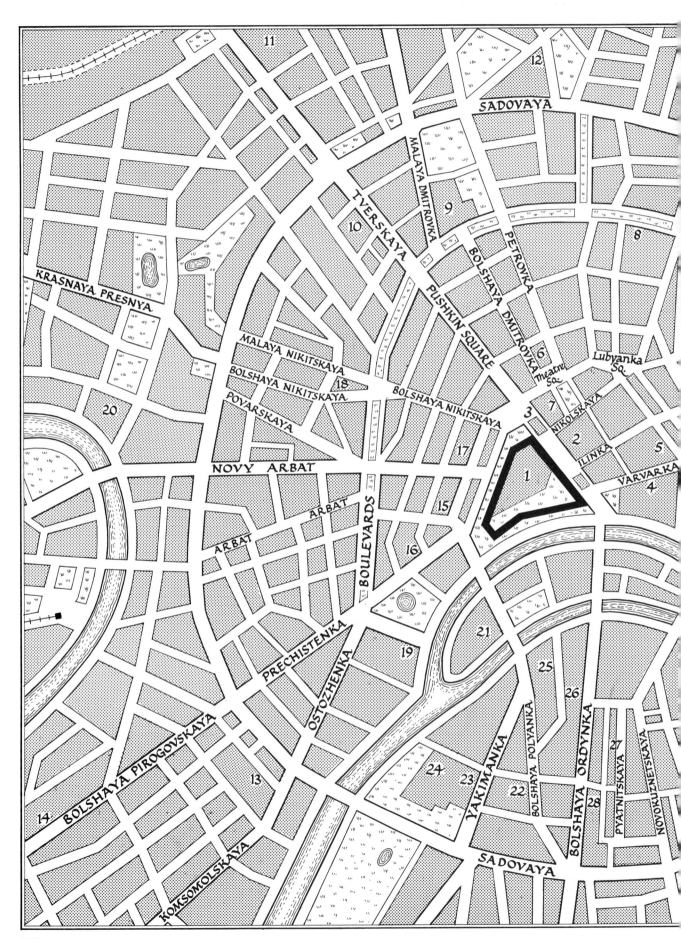

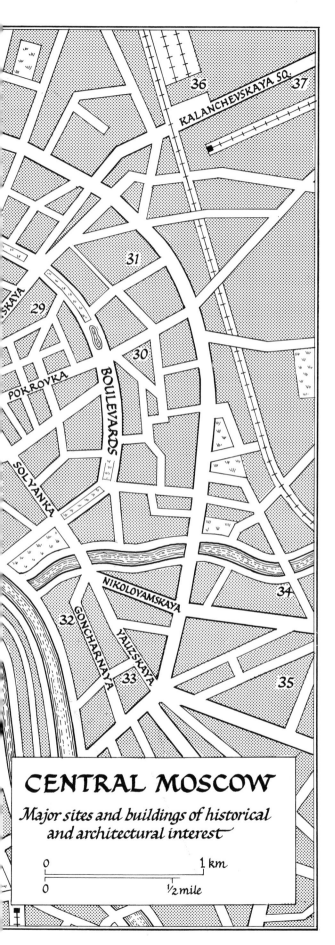

1. Kremlin
2. Red Square
3. History Museum
4. Old English Embassy
5. Church of the Trinity 'v Nikitnikah'
6. Bolshoi Theatre
7. Lenin Museum — DUMA
8. Nativity Convent
9. Church of the Nativity 'v Putinkakh'
10. Museum of the Revolution
11. St Nicholas, Old Believers
12. Red Army Theatre
13. St Nicholas 'v Kamovnikakh'
14. New Maidens (Novodevichy) Convent
15. Pashkov Museum
16. Pushkin Museum
17. House of Friendship
18. Large Church of the Ascension
19. Pertsov Apartment House
20. White House
21. Kirillov Church of St Nicholas and house
22. Igumnov Mansion
23. St John the Warrior
24. New Tretyakov Gallery
25. Old Tretyakov Gallery
26. Church of Our Lady of All Sorrows
27. St Nicholas 'v Pyzakh'
28. Community of Martha and Mary
29. Menshikov Tower
30. Apraxin-Trubetskoi Mansion
31. Yusupov Palace
32. St Nikita 'shto za Yauzu'
33. Potter's Church of the Assumption
34. Andronikov Monastery
35. Church of the Nativity 'v Starom Simonove'
36. Nikolai, Kazan and Yaroslavl Railway Stations
37. Rusakov Club

# Index